AAT
INTERACTIVE TEXT

Foundation Unit 22

Health, Safety and Security

September 2000 edition

This new Interactive Text for Unit 22 Health, Safety and Security is designed to be easy on the eye and easy to use.

- Clear language and presentation

- Lots of diagrams

- Practical examples

- Icons marking important areas

- Numerous activities

The text fully reflects the new standards for Unit 22. It is up to date with developments in subject matter as at 1 August 2000.

BPP Publishing
September 2000

First edition September 2000

ISBN 0 7517 6236 9

British Library Cataloguing-in-Publication Data
A catalogue record for this book
is available from the British Library

Published by

BPP Publishing Limited
Aldine House, Aldine Place
London W12 8AW

www.bpp.com

Printed in Great Britain by W M Print
Frederick Street
Walsall
West Midlands WS2 9NE

We are grateful to the Auditing Practices Board for permission to reproduce the glossary of auditing terms.

We are also grateful to the Lead Body for Accounting for permission to reproduce extracts from the Standards of Competence for Accounting, and to the AAT for permission to reproduce extracts from the mapping and Guidance Notes.

Contents

BPP PUBLISHING

HOW TO USE THIS INTERACTIVE TEXT

Aims of this Interactive Text

> To provide the knowledge and practice to help you succeed in the devolved assessment for Foundation Unit 22 *Monitor and Maintain a Healthy, Safe and Secure Workplace.*

> To provide underpinning knowledge and understanding for Foundation generally.

To pass the devolved assessments you need a thorough understanding in all areas covered by the standards of competence.

> **Interactive Text**
>
> This covers all you need to know for the devolved assessment for Unit 22 *Monitor and Maintain a Healthy, Safe and Secure Workplace.* Icons clearly mark key areas of the text. Numerous activities throughout the text help you practise what you have just learnt. This Text also covers certain information common to Foundation.

Recommended approach to this Interactive Text

(a) To achieve competence in Units 22 (and all the other units), you need to be able to do **everything** specified by the standards. Study the Interactive Text carefully and do not skip any of it.

(b) Learning is an **active** process. Do **all** the activities as you work through the Interactive Text so you can be sure you really understand what you have read.

(c) Before you take the devolved assessment, check that you still remember the material using the following quick revision plan for each chapter.

   (i) Read through the chapter learning objectives. Are there any gaps in your knowledge? If so, study the section again.

   (ii) Read and learn the key terms.

   (iii) Look at the devolved assessment alerts. These show the sort of things that are likely to come up.

   (iv) Read and learn the key learning points, which are a summary of the chapter.

   (v) Do the quick quiz again. If you know what you're doing, it shouldn't take long.

   This approach is only a suggestion. Your college may well adapt it to suit your needs.

Remember this is a **practical** course.

(a) Try to relate the material to your experience in the workplace or any other work experience you may have had.

(b) Try to make as many links as you can to your study of the other Units at Foundation level.

(c) Keep this text, (hopefully) you will find it invaluable in your everyday work too!

BPP PUBLISHING

FOUNDATION QUALIFICATION STRUCTURE

The competence-based Education and Training Scheme of the Association of Accounting Technicians is based on an analysis of the work of accounting staff in a wide range of industries and types of organisation. The Standards of Competence for Accounting which students are expected to meet are based on this analysis.

The Standards identify the key purpose of the accounting occupation, which is to operate, maintain and improve systems to record, plan, monitor and report on the financial activities of an organisation, and a number of key roles of the occupation. Each key role is subdivided into units of competence, which are further divided into elements of competences. By successfully completing assessments in specified units of competence, students can gain qualifications at NVQ/SVQ levels 2, 3 and 4, which correspond to the AAT Foundation, Intermediate and Technician stages of competence respectively.

Whether you are competent in a Unit is demonstrated by means of:

- *Either* a Central Assessment (set and marked by AAT assessors)

- *Or* a Devolved Assessment (where competence is judged by an Approved Assessment Centre to whom responsibility for this is devolved)

- Or *both* Central *and* Devolved Assessment

Below we set out the overall structure of the Foundation (NVQ/SVQ Level 2) stage, indicating how competence in each Unit is assessed.

NVQ/SVQ Level 2 - Foundation (All units are mandatory)

Unit of competence

Elements of competence

Unit 1	Recording income and receipts

1.1	Process documents relating to goods and services supplied
1.2	Receive and record receipts

Unit 2	Making and recording payments

2.1	Process documents relating to goods and services received
2.2	Prepare authorised payments
2.3	Make and record payments

Unit 3	Preparing ledger balances and an initial trial balance

3.1	Balance bank transactions
3.2	Prepare ledger balances and control accounts
3.3	Draft an initial trial balance

Unit 4	Supplying information for management control

4.1	Code and extract information
4.2	Provide comparisons on costs and income

Unit 20	Working with information technology

20.1	Input, store and output data
20.2	Minimise risks to data held on a computer system

Unit 22	Monitor and maintain a healthy safe and secure workplace (ASC)

22.1	Monitor and maintain health and safety within the workplace
22.2	Monitor and maintain the security of the workplace

Unit 23	Achieving personal effectiveness

23.1	Plan and organise own work
23.2	Establish and maintain working relationships
23.3	Maintain accounting files and records

UNIT 22 STANDARDS OF COMPETENCE

The structure of the Standards for Unit 22

The Unit commences with a statement of the **knowledge and understanding** which underpin competence in the Unit's elements.

The Unit of Competence is then divided into **elements of competence** describing activities which the individual should be able to perform.

Each element includes:

(a) **A** set of **performance criteria.** This defines what constitutes competent performance.

(b) A **range statement.** This defines the situations, contexts, methods etc in which competence should be displayed.

(c) **Evidence requirements.** These state that competence must be demonstrated consistently, over an appropriate time scale with evidence of performance being provided from the appropriate sources.

(d) **Sources of evidence.** These are suggestions of ways in which you can find evidence to demonstrate that competence. These fall under the headings: 'observed performance; work produced by the candidate; authenticated testimonies from relevant witnesses; personal account of competence; other sources of evidence.'

The elements of competence for Unit 22 are set out below. Knowledge and understanding required for the unit as a whole are listed first, followed by the performance criteria and range statements for each element. Performance criteria are cross-referenced below to chapters in this Text.

Unit 22: Monitor and Maintain a Healthy, Safe and Secure Workplace

What is the unit about?

This unit is about the individual's ability to monitor the workplace to minimise risks to self and others and to maintain a healthy and safe working environment. This includes the identification and rectification, when authorised and competent, of potential hazards and emergencies and adherence to legal and other regulations relating to safe and healthy work practices. Also included is following set procedures for the security of the premises and its contents, identifying security risks and taking appropriate action.

Elements contained within this unit are:

Element: 22.1   Monitor and Maintain Health and Safety Within the Workplace

Element: 22.2   Monitor and Maintain the Security of the Workplace

Knowledge and understanding

- Common forms of accident/health emergency (Element 22.1)

- Types and uses of fire and emergency equipment (Element 22.1)

- Hazards in the use of equipment (Element 22.1)

- Methods of minimising hazards in the work area (Element 22.1)

- Organisation's procedures for dealing with emergencies (Element 22.1)

- Own scope and limitations for dealing with emergencies (Element 22.1)

- Methods of reporting emergencies (Element 22.1 & 22.2)

- Relevant legal requirements (Element 22.1)

- Location of fire and emergency equipment (Element 22.1)

- Identification of potential security risks (Element 22.1)

- Organisation's security procedures (Element 22.1)

- Own scope and limitations for dealing with security risks (Element 22.1)

Element 22.1 Monitor and Maintain Health and Safety within the Workplace

Performance criteria	Chapters in this Text
1 Existing or potential hazards are put right if authorised	1
2 Hazards outsider own authority to put right are promptly and accurately reported to the appropriate person	1
3 Actions taken in dealing with emergencies conform to organisational requirements	1
4 Emergencies are reported and recorded accurately, completely and legibly in accordance with established procedures	1
5 Work practices are in accordance with organisational requirements	1
6 Working conditions which do not conform to organisational requirements are promptly and accurately reported to the appropriate person	1
7 Organising of work area minimises risk to self and others	1

Range statement

1 **Workplace:** all equipment, fixtures and fittings within own area of responsibility; all areas within the organisation

2 **Emergencies:** illness; accidents; fire; evacuation

3 **Organisational requirements:** instructions provided by the organisation to ensure compliance with legal requirements and codes of practice.

BPP PUBLISHING

Element 22.2 Monitor and Maintain the Security of the Workplace

Performance criteria	Chapters in this Text
1 Organisational security procedures are carried out correctly	2
2 Security risks are correctly identified	2
3 Identified security risks are out right or reported promptly to the appropriate person	2
4 Identified breaches of security are dealt with in accordance with organisational procedures	2

Range statement

1   **Security systems:** personal identification; entry; exit; equipment

ASSESSMENT STRATEGY

This unit is assessed by **devolved assessment**.

Devolved Assessment

Devolved assessment is a means of collecting evidence of your ability to carry out practical activities and to **operate effectively in the conditions of the workplace** to the standards required. Evidence may be collected at your place of work or at an Approved Assessment Centre by means of simulations of workplace activity, or by a combination of these methods.

If the Approved Assessment Centre is a **workplace** you may be observed carrying out accounting activities as part of your normal work routine. You should collect documentary evidence of the work you have done, or contributed, in an **accounting portfolio**. Evidence collected in a portfolio can be assessed in addition to observed performance or where it is not possible to assess by observation.

Where the Approved Assessment Centre is a **college or training organisation**, devolved assessment will be by means of a combination of the following.

(a)   Documentary evidence of activities carried out at the workplace, collected by you in an **accounting portfolio**

(b)   Realistic **simulations** of workplace activities; these simulations may take the form of case studies and in-tray exercises and involve the use of primary documents and reference sources

(c)   **Projects and assignments** designed to assess the Standards of Competence

If you are unable to provide workplace evidence, you will be able to complete the assessment requirements by the alternative methods listed above.

1 Health and safety at work

This chapter contains

1   Introduction: Why bother with health and safety?

2   Legal aspects of health and safety

3   Identifying and minimising hazards

4   Fire safety

5   Emergency procedures

6   Reporting procedures

Learning objectives

On completion of this chapter you will be able to:

- Put right existing or potential hazards, if authorised
- Report hazards outside your authority to the appropriate person
- Deal with emergencies in accordance with organisational requirements
- Report and record emergencies accurately, completely and legibly in accordance with established procedures
- Comply in all work practices with organisational requirements
- Report work conditions which do not conform to organisational requirements promptly and accurately to the appropriate person
- Organise your own work area to minimise risk to yourself and others
- Discuss common forms of accident/health emergency
- Describe types and uses of fire and emergency equipment
- Identify and know how to minimise potential hazards
- Outline the organisation's procedures for dealing with emergencies, and location and use of fire and emergency equipment
- Understand your own scope and limitations for dealing with emergencies
- Understand available methods of reporting emergencies
- Outline relevant legal requirements

BPP PUBLISHING

Performance criteria

(1) Existing or potential hazards are put right if authorised

(2) Hazards outside own authority to put right are promptly and accurately reported to the appropriate person

(3) Actions taken in dealing with emergencies conform to organisational requirements

(4) Emergencies are reported and recorded accurately, completely and legibly in accordance with established procedures

(5) Work practices are in accordance with organisational requirements

(6) Working conditions, which do not conform to organisational requirements, are promptly and accurately reported to the appropriate person

(7) Organising of work area minimised risk to self and others

Range statement

1 **Workplace:** all equipment, fixtures and fittings within own area of responsibility; all areas within the organisation

2 **Emergencies:** illness; accidents; fire; evacuation

3 **Organisational requirements:** instruction provided by the organisation to ensure compliance with legal requirements and codes of practice

Knowledge and understanding

- Common forms of accident/health emergency (Element 22.1)

- Types and uses of fire equipment (Element 22.1)

- Hazards in the use of equipment (Element 22.1)

- Methods of minimising hazards in the work area (Element 22.1)

- Organisation's procedures for dealing with emergencies (Element 22.1)

- Own scope and limitations for dealing with emergencies (Element 22.1)

- Methods of reporting emergencies (Element 22.1)

- Relevant legal requirements (Element 22.1)

- Location of fire and emergency equipment (Element 22.1)

- Identification of potential security risks (Element 22.1)

- Organisation's security procedures (Element 22.1)

- Own scope and limitations for dealing with security risks (Element 22.1)

1 INTRODUCTION: WHY BOTHER WITH HEALTH AND SAFETY?

1.1 You could probably make your own list of reasons for operating safely in the workplace.

(a) Obviously, and most importantly, to protect yourself and others from **dangers** that might cause injury or sickness.

(b) Sickness, accidents and injuries **cost money**.

(c) Employees, as well as employers, have **legal obligations** to observe health and safety requirements. (We'll discuss these in Section 2 below.)

Risks in the office

1.2 You perhaps associate risk in the workplace with building sites or factories with heavy machinery or coal mines, but assuming you work in an **office** of some sort you need only look about you to find many potential **sources of injury** or **ill-health**.

- Slippery or uneven floors

- Frayed carpets

- Trailing electric leads, telephone cables and other wires

- Obstacles (boxes, files, books, open drawers) in gangways

- Standing on chairs (particularly swivel chairs) to reach high shelving

- Blocked staircases, for example where they are used for extra storage space

- Lifting heavy items without bending properly.

- Removing the safety guard on a machine to free a blockage or to make it run faster.

- Using chemicals without protective clothing or adequate ventilation.

- Taking inadequate work breaks, allowing excessive exposure or strain.

1.3 Sometimes none of these things are needed to cause an accident: it is very easy to do it without props! **Carelessness** or **foolishness** are major causes of accidents, and you need to remember that you are responsible for your own behaviour at work. Practical jokes and 'cutting corners' in work practices can have unforeseen consequences!

DEVOLVED ASSESSMENT ALERT

Don't think of health and safety as purely a legal or procedural matter! You need to be able to demonstrate an awareness of how everyday working practices, the working environment and the behaviour of people can put you and others at risk. (This unit is about the individual's ability to monitor the workplace to minimise risk to self and others and to maintain a healthy and safe working environment.)

Accidents and illness cost money

1.4 More than 700,000 people are injured at work in Britain every year, and the Health and Safety Executive estimate that the real **cost of work-related ill health, accidents and injury** equates to between five and ten percent of Britain's gross trading profit every year, an average of £170 - £360 per employed person.

Activity 1.1

What might be the cost to you, the employee, of a serious accident or illness at work?

1.5 **Costs to the employer**

- **Productive time lost** by the absent employee

- Productive time lost by **other employees** who (through choice or necessity) stop work at the time of, or following, the accident

- A proportion of the cost of employing **first aid and medical staff**

- The cost of **disruption** to operations at work

- The cost of any **damage to the equipment** or any cost associated with the subsequent **modification** of the equipment

- The cost of any **compensation payments or fines** resulting from legal action following an accident

- The costs associated with **increased insurance premiums**

- **Reduced output** from the injured employee on return to work

- The cost of possible **reduced morale,** increased absenteeism or increased labour turnover among employees

- The cost of **recruiting and training a replacement** for the absent employee

2 LEGAL ASPECTS OF HEALTH AND SAFETY

2.1 In the UK there are several Acts of Parliament applying to workplaces. The UK has also implemented six EC directives on various aspects of health and safety by issuing new **Regulations** and **Codes of Practice** under the **Health and Safety at Work Act 1974.** Regulations are legally enforceable, but Codes of Practice do not have to be followed to the letter. They are more like the Highway Code in the sense that failure to comply with them is *indicative* of failure of a legal duty in this context to provide a safe and healthy place of work. Some of the main provisions will be discussed in this section.

DEVOLVED ASSESSMENT ALERT

You are not expected to have a detailed knowledge of health and safety law, but you *do* need to be able to monitor and fulfil organisational procedures and instructions designed to ensure compliance with relevant legal requirements and codes of practice. The following background will help you to evaluate and fulfil these organisational requirements - but make sure you know exactly what your employer's health and safety rules and procedures are.

2.2 We need to look mainly at the **legal duties of the employer.** This is not so that you can police him or threaten him with prosecution, but simply so that you know what a safe and healthy workplace is supposed to be. Employers are obliged to designate specifically one or more competent workers to assist them in undertaking protective and preventative measures. If this topic interests you, you could consider putting yourself forward as such an assistant. Firstly, though, be aware that *you* have certain obligations.

Duties of employees regarding health and safety

2.3 You have a general **responsibility not to cause harm** to other people or property wherever you are - walking down the street, attending a lecture, working at your desk or sitting at home in front of the TV. You are guilty of a crime and/or a tort if you damage other people or property.

2.4 As an *employee*, you are obliged under the **Health and Safety at Work Act 1974** to:

- Take **reasonable care** to avoid injury to yourself and others

- **Co-operate** with your employer to help him comply with his legal obligations

2.5 Under the **Management of Health and Safety at Work Regulations 1992** you have the added responsibility to:

- Use all equipment, safety devices, etc, provided by your employer **properly** and in accordance with the instructions and training received

- **Inform** your employer, or another employee with specific responsibility for health and safety, of any perceived shortcoming in safety arrangements or any serious and immediate dangers to health and safety.

2.6 If an employee **flouts safety regulations** (whether or not an accident actually occurs) he can be prosecuted and fined up to £20,000 or, for very serious cases, he can be fined without limit or imprisoned. If he himself is injured he may be refused compensation because he brought the injuries upon himself. Even if the case does not go to court, the guilty employee may face disciplinary action by his employer.

Duties of employers: safety policy

2.7 The **Health and Safety at Work Act 1974** imposes specific duties upon employers to make sure that all systems (that is, work practices) are safe, that the work environment is safe and healthy (see below) and that plant and equipment is kept up to the necessary standard. Regulations issued under the authority of this Act require the employer to do the following.

(a) Produce a **written statement of his safety measures** and the means used to implement them. This statement should be brought to the notice of his employees. An employer who has less than five employees is exempt from this requirement.

(b) **Consult with safety representatives** appointed by recognised trade unions with a view to the effective maintenance of adequate safety measures.

(c) Appoint a **safety committee** if requested to do so by the safety representatives, to keep safety measures under review.

2.8 Under the **Management of Health and Safety at Work Regulations 1992** employers must:

(a) Carry out **risk assessment**, generally in writing, of all work hazards on a continuous basis

(b) Introduce **controls** to reduce risks

(c) Assess the **risks to anyone else** affected by their work activities

(d) **Share hazard and risk information** with other employers, including those on adjoining premises, other site occupiers and all subcontractors coming onto the premises

(e) Should revise **safety policies** in the light of the above, or initiate safety policies if none were in place previously

(f) **Identify employees who are especially at risk**

(g) Provide up-to-date and appropriate **training in safety matters**

(h) Provide **information** to employees (including temps) about health and safety

(i) Employ **competent safety and health advisers**

Activity 1.2

Consider the health and safety programme at your place of work (or study).

(a) How well *aware* are you of any rules, procedures and information regarding health and safety? (Who is responsible for *making* you more aware of such matters?)

(b) How well do the organisation's rules, procedures and information comply with the requirements of the Regulations?

2.9 Other legislation

(a) The **Health and Safety (Young Persons) Regulations 1997** require them to take into account the lack of experience, absence of awareness of existing or potential risks and/or the relative immaturity of young employees (aged under 18) when assessing the risks to their health and safety.

(b) The **Health and Safety (Safety Signs and Signals) Regulations 1996** describe the safety signs and signals that should be provided in the workplace and how they should be used and require employers to instruct employees on their use and meaning.

Duties of employers: the work environment

2.10 The **Offices, Shops and Railway Premises Act 1963** has a number of rules governing the environment in which employees work and these have been supplemented by the **Workplace (Health, Safety and Welfare) Regulations 1992**.

(a) **Cleanliness**

Floors and steps must be cleaned at least once a week. Furniture and fittings must be kept clean. Rubbish must not be allowed to accumulate in work areas. This, of course, means not only paper but also food debris and so on.

(b) **Overcrowding**

Each person should have at least 11 cubic metres of space, ignoring any parts of rooms more than 3.1 metres above the floor or with a headroom of less than 2.0 metres. This sounds like quite a lot of space, but it is not much more than the space occupied by your desk and chair and a passageway around it sufficient to allow you to get in and out.

(c) **Ventilation**

There must be an adequate supply of fresh or purified air in circulation.

(d) **Temperature**

A reasonable temperature must be maintained (except for brief periods). The minimum is 16°C where people are sitting down, or 13°C if they move about to do their work. A thermometer must be provided on each floor on permanent display.

(e) **Lighting and windows**

There must be adequate natural or artificial light (preferably natural, if practicable). Windows must be kept clean inside and out and lighting equipment must be properly maintained. Windows should be made of safe materials and if they are openable it should be possible to do this safely.

(f) **Toilets**

There must be enough suitable toilets and they must be properly ventilated and lit, kept clean and properly maintained. Broadly speaking, enough means a Gents and Ladies WC for every 15 to 20 employees.

(g) **Washing facilities**

These should be provided on the same scale as toilets. They should have clean hot and cold water, soap and towels or the equivalent.

(h) **Drinking water**

Adequate drinking water must be provided together with cups or a fountain.

(i) **Clothing**

There should be somewhere to hang up outdoor clothing and facilities for drying it. Facilities for changing clothing should be available where appropriate.

(j) **Seating**

Seats must be provided for rest periods, and, where work can or must be done sitting down, seats must be suitable in design, construction and dimensions.

(k) **Eating facilities**

Suitable facilities must be available for workers who eat in the workplace. Normally a desk in an office would be regarded as suitable.

(l) **Lifts**

Lifts must be safe. They must be examined by a competent engineer at least every 6 months.

(m) **Floors, passages and stairs**

These should be soundly constructed and maintained, without holes, slip-free, and kept free from obstruction. Stairs should have hand-rails; floor openings should be fenced round.

(n) **Traffic routes**

These should have regard to the safety of pedestrians and vehicles alike.

(o) **Doors and gates**

These should be suitably constructed and fitted with any necessary safety devices (especially sliding doors and powered doors and doors opening in either direction).

(p) **Escalators and travelators**

These should function safely and have readily accessible emergency stop devices.

(q) **Machinery and equipment**

All equipment should be properly maintained. Dangerous parts of machines should be fenced. No person under the age of 18 should be required to clean machinery if this would expose him to risk, and no person should be allowed to operate a machine specified as dangerous unless fully instructed of the dangers. Equipment is discussed in more detail below.

(r) **Heavy lifting**

People should not be required to lift, carry or move a load likely to cause injury. This is further discussed below.

(s) **Falls or falling objects**

These should be prevented by erecting effective physical safeguards (fences, safety nets, ground rails and so on).

(t) **Fire precautions**

Appropriate fire-fighting equipment should be provided and there must be an adequate means of escape. Business premises should generally have a valid fire certificate from the local fire authority (though this depends on the number of floors and the number of people). Fire exits should be clearly marked and escape routes kept unobstructed. Fire alarms should be provided and tested periodically and people working in the building should be familiar with the escape drill.

(u) **First-aid**

A firstaid box or cupboard under the charge of a responsible person should be provided for every 150 employees or fraction thereof (there should be two if there are 160 employees). Where there are more than 150 employees the responsible person should be trained in first aid and should be available to attend to accidents during working hours. Where there are more than 400 employees there should be a first aid room.

2.11 Even if you are **working at home,** you are still an employee and so your employer is required to provide you with a safe place of work, just as he has to for those employees working at his actual premises.

Duties of employers: first aid

2.12 The **Health and Safety (First Aid) Regulations 1981** require employers to provide adequate and appropriate equipment, facilities and personnel to enable first aid to be given to employees if they are injured or become ill at work. The minimum contents that should be found in a first aid box, for example, consist of dressings (plasters) and bandages of various sizes.

2.13 There are also certain items that should **not be kept in a first aid box**, including:

• Tablets	• Scissors
• Creams	• Tweezers
• Lotions	• Eyewashes
• Potions	

These must not be offered or administered to employees even if requested.

2.14 This does not mean that you can't take a paracetamol tablet at work if you have a headache. However, it is **your responsibility** to provide yourself with what is appropriate. If you are allergic to a particular drug *you* are expected to have the sense not to take it.

Duties of employers: consultation with employees

2.15 Under the **Safety Representatives and Safety Committees Regulations 1977** and the **Health and Safety (Consultation with Employees) Regulations 1996**, employers must consult all of their employees on health and safety matters (such as the planning of health and safety training, any change in equipment or procedures which may substantially affect their health and safety at work or the health and safety consequences of introducing new technology). This involves giving information to employees *and* listening to and taking account of what they say before any health and safety decisions are taken.

Activity 1.3

A quick quiz! Under health and safety legislation there are certain requirements for workplace conditions. In your own words, briefly state the requirements under each of the following headings.

(a) Temperature
(b) Eating facilities
(c) Room dimensions
(d) Lighting
(e) Ventilation
(f) Equipment
(g) Sanitary conveniences

3 IDENTIFYING AND MINIMISING HAZARDS

KEY TERMS

A **hazard** is a thing likely to cause injury, or a point of exposure to risk of accident, injury or loss.

3.1 In order to **minimise hazards** in the workplace, employers will need to assess the likely risk to the workforce from things such as the equipment and the machinery used by its employees and also the layout of the office in which the employees work.

DEVOLVED ASSESSMENT ALERT

The evidence requirements for Element 22.1 state that: 'Performance evidence must be available of the candidate **identifying** potential hazards and emergencies in the workplace, and taking appropriate action, in accordance with organisational requirements.'

Do not hesitate to check your workplace and work practices against the potential hazards described in this section.

Office equipment

3.2 You are expected to be able to use equipment as laid down in **operating instructions**. In practice you will probably be shown how to use office equipment like the photocopier, the fax machine and the computer printers in your first few days in a job. It is when you first encounter difficulties that you need to be careful.

3.3   It will not be long before you are the one using the photocopier when it runs out of paper or your print-out gets chewed up by the printer because the paper is not feeding through correctly. Obviously if you have not been shown what to do in these circumstances you should **ask somebody who knows**.

3.4   If you are likely to be using the equipment in question a good deal, **read the operating manual** and learn how to deal with routine problems.

Electrical equipment

3.5   Many of the items of equipment found in the workplace these days are electrical. The following adaptation from a photocopier instruction manual is designed to demonstrate the kind of **precautions which should be taken when operating any electrical equipment**.

3.6   **General rules that apply when operating any electrical equipment**

(a)   Never place **heavy objects** on the equipment, or subject it to shocks.

(b)   **Insert the plug fully** into the electrical socket. Do not use damaged plugs or sockets.

(c)   **Do not remove or open any covers** while using the equipment.

(d)   If the equipment becomes **jammed**, follow the instruction manual for unjamming. Be sure to turn the equipment off if the information manual tells you to do so.

(e)   Never **unplug or turn off** the equipment while it is in operation.

(f)   When unplugging the power cord, do not pull on the cord. **Grasp the plug** and pull it out.

(g)   If the plug or the socket get hot, **switch off at the socket**, pull out the plug and call a qualified electrician.

(h)   Never bring any **magnetised object** near the equipment.

(i)   Never use **inflammable aerosols or liquids** near the equipment.

(j)   Never place a **vessel containing water** on the equipment.

(k)   Be careful not to **drop paper clips, staples or other small objects** into the equipment.

(l)   If the equipment produces smoke, becomes inordinately hot, or produces abnormal noises, turn it off, unplug it and then **call your local dealer** immediately.

(m)   Turn the equipment off at the **end of the workday** or during a power blackout.

(n)   **Do not plug the equipment into the same power outlet** being used for other electrical equipment.

(o)   Watch out especially for **exposed wires**: stress points like the base of the plug and the point where the flex enters the equipment are particularly dangerous.

3.7   If the worst happens and someone receives an **electric shock** you should stop the current if possible by switching off at the wall or pulling out the plug. If this is not possible you should stand on a dry surface (a piece of wood or a newspaper is ideal) and knock the part of the victim's body clear of the source of the electricity using something non-conductive like a piece of wood, or a rolled up newspaper - *not* metal. Avoid anything wet and do not touch the person's body with your own until the current is switched off.

Activity 1.4

Your company has just purchased some laser printers manufactured in the USA to replace its old dot matrix printers. An extract from the manual is shown below. Read it carefully.

Laser safety

This printer is complied with 21 CFR Chapter 1 Subchapter J as a Class 1 laser product under the US Department of Health and Human Services (DHHS) Radiation Performance Standard according to the Radiation Control for Health and Safety Act 1968. This means that the printer does not produce hazardous laser radiation.

Since radiation emitted inside the printer is completely confined within protective housings and external covers, the laser beam cannot escape from the machine during any phase of user operation.

FCC Regulations

This equipment generates and uses radio frequency energy, and if not installed and used properly, that is, in strict accordance with the manufacturer's instructions, may cause interference to radio and television reception. It has been type-tested and found to comply with the limits for a Class B computing device in accordance with the specifications in Subpart J of Part 15 of the FCC rules, which are designed to provide reasonable protection against such interference in a residential installation.

*DOC * regulations*

This digital apparatus does not exceed the Class B limits for radio noise emissions from digital apparatus set out in Radio Interference Regulations of the Canadian Department of Communications.

* DOC: Canadian Department of Communications.

Regulations for United Kingdom

This equipment is approved under approval number NS/G/23/J/100003 for indirect connection to public telecommunication systems in the United Kingdom, ie when connected to the correct interface of a type approved apparatus in accordance with the instructions for use of that apparatus. If you are uncertain about the connection arrangement, seek the help of a qualified engineer.

For ozone emission

This printer meets the requirements for ozone emission of the applicable standard published by Underwriters' Laboratories, Inc (UL). Ozone is a colourless gas (O_3), a by-product of the electrophotographic process. Ozone is only discharged while the printer is printing, and it is emitted through the exhaust port on the rear, left side of the printer.

Caution

Those who are particularly sensitive to ozone odour may rarely feel sick if exposed to it excessively. To avoid this, make sure that the following measures are taken.

- Install the printer in a well ventilated room. (Ventilate about every hour or choose a large room.)
- Avoid using multiple laser printers simultaneously.
- Avoid facing the exhaust port directly towards the users.
- Replace a disposable ozone filter every 100,000 pages.
- Avoid using the printer without a filter.

BPP PUBLISHING

Required

Frederick thinks lasers are dangerous and is therefore very worried about these new laser printers. How would you reassure him that the printer can be operated safely?

Mechanical equipment

3.8 Basic **office tools** also need care: devices designed to puncture or cut paper or plastic are just as good at making holes and gashes in flesh! Beware of guillotines, scissors, hole punches, binding machines, franking machines, letter openers and staplers. Anything, in fact, but especially anything with a point or a sharp edge or which works by impact, is capable of causing an injury if it is misused or even if it is left lying unguarded. Don't forget, also, that electricity and moving parts generate heat. A machine that is left ticking over all day may get *very* hot.

3.9 Be particularly careful with **personal effects** like necklaces, bracelets or other jewellery, and ties and scarves, all of which are inclined to get trapped in machines with moving parts. Long hair can also be a hazard: you may prefer to tie it back in some way if you feel it is particularly at risk because of machinery you use.

3.10 **Vibration White Finger** (VWF) is a painful condition which may be developed by regular users of hand-operated tools and machinery which produce high levels of vibration. The disease is estimated to affect around 20,000 people, with 1,400 new cases being reported each year. The risk of developing the condition can be reduced in a number of ways.

- Use the **right tool** for the job.
- Keep tools and machinery in **good working order** to minimise vibration.
- Avoid using machinery for long periods without a **break**.

DEVOLVED ASSESSMENT ALERT

'Phasing work activities to minimise risk to self' is one of the cited sources of evidence for this element: it means pacing yourself and taking breaks, so far as you have authority to do so. Be aware of how your work patterns and hours can cause or minimise risks such as exposure to VDUs, VWF (discussed above), RSI (discussed below), tiredness and loss of concentration (which may lead to accidents) and so on.

Chemicals

3.11 Some items of equipment and machinery may need liquid or powder additives: beware of corrosive or toxic chemicals, flammable substances such as spirit or oil, and anything that gives off fumes. **Tippex** is harmful if it is inhaled or swallowed or comes into contact with your eyes. Sniffing **glue** or other solvents can be fatal.

3.12 Containers should be clearly labelled with their contents and warning signs as appropriate. If the **instructions** say wear protective gloves or wash off any splashes then do so!

3.13 The short-term effects of **breathing in harmful substances** can cause coughing, wheezing and shortness of breath. Long-term or high short-term exposure to substances like hay, wood dust and some glues can lead to chronic disablement from diseases like occupational asthma.

3.14   If skin comes into contact with substances such as shampoos, the sap from certain agricultural crops and cement, a serious and debilitating disease called **work-related dermatitis** can occur. Symptoms of the condition include redness, itching, scaling and blistering of the skin. The skin can crack and bleed and the dermatitis can spread all over the body. It can be painful enough to keep people off work or even force them to change jobs. The disease is most widespread among industries such as hairdressing, catering and cleaning.

3.15   Certain chemicals which are used in the workplace have the potential to cause cancer and it is estimated that about 6,000 deaths a year (of which 3,000 are caused by exposure to asbestos) are due to **work-related cancer**.

3.16   The **Control of Substances Hazardous to Health Regulations 1994** require employers to prevent or, if this is not possible, control employees' exposure to such substances.

3.17   If you or your organisation uses a harmful substance you should report any defects in **control measures** (such as local exhaust ventilation). Wear the respiratory protection that is provided and take care of it if you are likely to be breathing in a harmful substance. If you discover any material or dust which you suspect contains asbestos, stop any work that is being carried out and get advice. If you or your organisation uses asbestos material you should find out what precautions to take to protect health and make sure that they are followed.

Noise

3.18   As a general rule, if you have to shout to be clearly heard by someone two metres away then **noise** may well be a problem in your job. According to the Government, regular exposure to noise levels equivalent to the noise generated by a busy street over an eight-hour day is hazardous. Common sources of loud noise include pavement hammering, chainsaw work, sheet metal working and wood machinery. Poor maintenance, such as holes in compressed air lines and escaping steam, is also a cause of loud noise.

3.19   The **Noise at Work Regulations 1989** require workers to be protected from loud noise. Employers must therefore reduce noise levels as far as is reasonably practicable. If having done this the daily noise exposure level is equivalent to the noise of a heavy lorry, an employer must provide workers with ear protectors and mark the areas in which they should be worn.

3.20   **How to protect your hearing**

        (a)   Use **noise control equipment** provided by your employer.

        (b)   Tell your employer if something needs **repairing**.

        (c)   Don't remove from a machine any **equipment supplied for controlling noise**.

        (d)   Wear **ear protectors** provided and look after them; use them properly, keep them clean and replace damaged muffs.

Computer workstations and VDUs

3.21   Most office workers today use a computer.

3.22 If you have ever worked for a long period at a VDU you may personally have experienced some **discomfort**. Back ache, eye strain and stiffness or muscular problems of the neck, shoulders, arms or hands are frequent complaints.

KEY TERM

Repetitive Strain Injury or RSI is the common term for a condition that arises when you work for long periods at a VDU.

3.23 **Disorders seem to arise from poor equipment, environment and posture,** which lead to muscles being starved of oxygen, the build up of waste products in the body and the compression of nerves.

3.24 Workstations have to meet **stringent legal requirements**.

DEVOLVED ASSESSMENT ALERT

Two of the potential sources of evidence of your competence in this element is your observed behaviour in 'organising your own workstation to reduce hazards - reducing glare, positioning equipment, furniture and materials' and 'phasing your work activities to minimise risk to yourself - exposure to VDUs'. Take advantage of the following advice to make the most of the opportunities.

Activity 1.5

The main provisions of the **Health and Safety (Display Screen Equipment) Regulations 1992** are as follows. Tick them if your own workstation meets the criteria. If your workstation is not compliant in any area, try to suggest how it might be made compliant.

Item of equipment	Requirement	Is my workstation compliant?
VDU	It must not flicker, must be free from glare, and must swivel and tilt.	
Keyboard	It must tilt and must be free from glare; the workspace in front of it must be sufficient for you to rest your forearms.	
Desk	It must be free from glare; there must be enough space to allow flexible arrangement of all equipment and documents. Measurements are not specified.	
Chair	The seat must be adjustable in height, and the back in height and angle; footrests must be made available if required.	
Lighting	There must be appropriate contrast between the screen and its background; windows must have some form of blinds.	
Heat and humidity	Levels must be adequate on the one hand and not uncomfortable on the other.	
Radiation	This must be reduced to negligible levels.	
Breaks	Screen work must be periodically interrupted by breaks or changes in activity. Short, frequent breaks (say, five or ten minutes per hour) are better than longer breaks at longer intervals.	

Eyesight	The employer must offer **free eyesight testing** at regular intervals and provide any special glasses that may be needed for screen work.
Consultation	You must be consulted about health and safety measures.
Training	Training in the proper use of equipment must be provided.

3.25   The following diagram shows the recommended way of **sitting at a VDU** and of positioning the equipment.

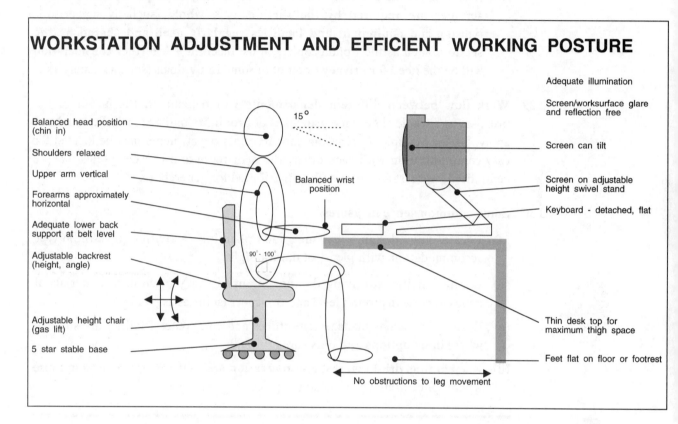

WORKSTATION ADJUSTMENT AND EFFICIENT WORKING POSTURE

Activity 1.6

You are normally quite fit but ever since you started working in your present office you have found that you have a slight backache when you wake up in the morning.

What sort of things might be causing your backache and what should you do to avoid straining your back in future?

Office layout

3.26   **Accidents** occur because people have to move about and do things within the office or factory environment. We will look briefly at hazards in the locations and methods by which people go about their work. This is to help you to recognise potential hazards in your own workplace, and understand when you or others may be at risk.

3.27   Office layout is determined by a number of considerations, such as **economy of space**, **efficiency** and **security**, but the **safety** of the occupants should not be forgotten. If there is insufficient **space** for people and equipment (and movement), there may be safety hazards, as movement is obstructed. Particular attention must be given to access to **emergency equipment** (such as fire extinguishers) and emergency exits, the ability to close **fire or security doors** and so on.

3.28 **Proximity and accessibility**

(a) Within each section, attention should be given to the **proximity** of people regularly working together (for example the manager and his/her secretary), and supervisors and those under their control.

(b) Attention should also be given to the **accessibility** of people **whose advice or services are required by the section as a whole** (such as supervisors, typists), and **equipment and facilities regularly used and shared by the section** (such as files, photocopier, coffee machine). A further consideration will be the **need for privacy or quiet** of some individuals (such as managers).

3.29 **Work flow between different departments** will depend on the layout of the premises as a whole. The same principles of **proximity** and **accessibility** ought to apply. So, for example, Purchasing and Accounts departments may be located for easy communication with each other; the mail room and office supplies may be centralised, and rest areas and toilets distributed for general use.

3.30 **Some common sense measures**

(a) Locate any design, drawing and planning activities in studio-type accommodation, with plenty of **natural light.**

(b) Locate activities involving the **movement** of heavy machinery, materials or goods as close to ground level and transport facilities as possible.

(c) Ensure that senior management offices and conference facilities are situated where **interruptions and noise** are minimal.

(d) Keep **dining, drinking, rest and recreation** areas (if any) separate from those where concentrated work is taking place.

Activity 1.7

What potential hazards would be minimised by the measures listed in paragraphs 3.27 and 3.28?

Your work area

3.31 In the light of the above look at **your own work area** - not just the desk you sit at but the corridors, passageways, staircases and so on that you use regularly as you go about your work.

	Suggested improvement
Do you often have to carry heavy files from one place to another?	Can you house often-used files in a cabinet within reach of your desk?
Do you have enough light for the work that you do?	Can you reorient your desk to take better advantage of natural light? Would a desk lamp help?

	Suggested improvement
What's the temperature like?	Do you have access to the air control switch or thermostat? Could you get agreement for a temperature adjustment from other people in the same area?
Do you have difficulty getting objects safely from shelves?	Make sure that heavy or unstable objects are at the bottom. (The same applies to liquids or chemicals.) Ask about the availability of a stable 'step up' aid to reaching higher shelves: chairs and step ladders are not ideal.
Are the things you need in easy reach?	Tidiness helps!
Is your chair comfortable and is your desk the right height?	If you often have backache or neckache, the height and contour of the chair probably need adjusting. Taking regular breaks and stretching or walking about are also recommended.

Each time you encounter an obstruction or potential hazard, **note it** - and come up with an **improvement plan**.

DEVOLVED ASSESSMENT ALERT

Remember that part of your competence is to demonstrate that you can spot potential hazards. Identifying – and *recording* your identification of – hazards in your own area is a great start!

Behaviour in work areas

Movement

3.32 You have known from painful experience since you were small that **sudden violent movements** in **confined spaces** are liable to cause damage. If you run past doorways, round blind corners or up or down stairways, if you throw objects across a room because you are too lazy to get up, if you wave your arms about, if you lean back on your chair too far, or if you stretch awkwardly to reach inaccessible files - if you do any of these things the chances are that *this time* you will come to no harm. But next time may be different. You are an accident waiting to happen. The same applies to **practical jokes** and '**clowning around**': it's all fun until someone loses an eye!

Alcohol and drugs

3.33 There may well be strict **drug and alcohol policies** in force in the workplace. Even if not, know your limit and recognise that any amount of alcohol is likely to impair your work performance and make you feel sleepy. It also lowers your concentration, awareness of risk, and reaction times: you are less safe when operating office equipment (let alone heavy machinery or motor vehicles!). The same may apply to prescription medications: be sensible about your capacity to work safely if you have taken drowsy-making painkillers or hayfever tablets. If in doubt, ask to be transferred to lower-risk duties, or consult your supervisor.

Smoking

3.34 Increasingly, firms are introducing a **non-smoking policy** in workplaces, often with the full support of staff, including smokers. There may be a complete ban or separate areas set aside for smokers during breaks. The health risk from **passive smoking** is well-publicised. There is also a fire risk, which may be magnified in offices where smoking is not normal and proper ashtrays and so on are not therefore available.

Activity 1.8

What are the policies of your workplace in regard to:

(a)　Drugs and alcohol?

(b)　Smoking?

If there is no formal policy statement: consider drafting one!

Heavy lifting

3.35 More than a quarter of accidents reported each year are associated with manual handling, back injuries being the most common. This activity is covered by the **Manual Handling Operations Regulations 1992**.

(a) Employers should **avoid the need for their employees to undertake any manual handling activities** which will involve the risk of their becoming injured, so far as this is reasonably practical.

(b) If such risks cannot be entirely avoided, employers should see to it that **information is available about the weight of each load** and the heavier side of any load whose centre or gravity is not positioned centrally.

(c) **Employees** then have a duty to take note of the information available and to make use of any equipment provided to help carry the load.

(d) Employees also have a duty to **inform their employer** of any injury or conditions that may affect their ability to undertake manual handling tasks.

Mental well-being

3.36 A hidden, but evidently very serious, source of potential hazard in the workplace is **Work-related stress**. Stress can be caused by a wide range of factors.

- Work overload; excessive work or pressure

- Work 'underload' - boredom, monotony and lack of meaning

- Poor management style: lack of clear instructions or targets, unpredictable moods and so on

- Lack of constructive relationships with colleagues: hostility, competition, 'cliques' and so on

- Insecurity, uncertainty; change over which the individual has no control

- Personality factors, such as emotional sensitivity, lack of flexibility, or perfectionism

- Non-work factors or circumstances: bereavement, illness, financial or relationship difficulties and so on

3.37 The **signs of harmful stress** include irritability and mood swings; sleeplessness; skin and digestive disorders and other physical symptoms; withdrawal; abuse of drugs or alcohol; apathy and low confidence; and changes in behaviour at work (eg unusually poor timekeeping or error rates).

Activity 1.9

Who would be the appropriate person to ask about **managing workplace stress** in your organisation (or outside it)? Selecting an appropriate communication method, request information on how to manage stress.

Risk assessment

3.38 The principal aim of the Health and Safety Executive is to ensure that health and safety risks from work activities are properly controlled. In order to do this, risks must be assessed:

Step 1	Look for hazards
Step 2	Decide who might be harmed, and how
Step 3	Evaluate risks arising and decide if existing precautions are adequate
Step 4	Record your findings
Step 5	Review your assessment periodically and revise as necessary

---

Activity 1.10

A scene from everyday office life is shown on the next page.

Note down anything that strikes you as being dangerous about this working environment.

BPP PUBLISHING

4 FIRE SAFETY

Safety procedures: fire

4.1 The general regulations relating to fire contained in the **Offices, Shops and Railway Premises Act 1963** were reinforced in the **Fire Precautions Act 1971.** (Specialised buildings are covered by other legislation such as the Fire Safety and Safety of Places of Sport Act 1987.) More recently, European legislation was implemented in the **Fire Precautions (Workplace) Regulations 1997**, which require employers to do the following.

(a) Provide the appropriate number of **fire extinguishers** and other means for fighting fire.

(b) Install **fire detectors** and **fire alarm systems** where necessary.

(c) Take whatever measures are necessary for **fighting fire** (eg the drawing up of a suitable emergency plan of action) and nominate a sufficient number of workers to implement these measures and ensure that they are adequately trained and equipped to carry out their responsibilities.

(d) Provide adequate **emergency routes and exits** for everyone to escape quickly and safely.

(e) Ensure that **equipment and facilities provided to protect workers** from the dangers of fire are regularly maintained and any faults found are rectified as quickly as possible.

KEY TERM

Fire equipment and facilities include **fire doors, fire notices, fire alarms, fire extinguishers** and **sprinklers.**

Causes of fire

4.2   The main causes of fire in industry and commerce tend to be associated with **electrical appliances and installations,** and **smoking** is a major source of fires in business premises.

4.3   **Flammable materials** like clothing and some furniture are a danger, particularly in an office which is heated by electric bar fires. **Flammable substances** left in the wrong place can also be a problem, for example if an aerosol is left in direct sunlight.

Activity 1.11

As with identifying hazards in your own workstation, see if you are up to speed with fire safety in your office.

Area	Am I competent?
Do you know what to do if fire breaks out in your workplace?	
Would you recognise the sound of a smoke alarm or fire alarm for what it was?	
Where is the nearest fire extinguisher?	
How do you set off the fire alarm?	
Where is the nearest fire exit?	
Where is the meeting point in case of evacuation?	
Should you leave doors open or shut?	
Does anybody know at any given time when you are (or are not) in the building?	
Who is the Fire/Safety officer?	

4.4   The notices below provide some fire safety information, but it is more important that you take note of the **fire safety policy** within your own office.

Carbon Dioxide Fire Extinguisher

2kg stored pressure type for class B fires liquid and electrical equipment

Use upright

Pull out pin

Lift horn aim at base of fire

Squeeze handles

Recharge after complete or partial use
Temperature range 20°C to 60°C
Fire test rating 34B

Model No. TG97

Lic. No. 7284

Fire Extinguisher

9 litre gas cartridge type for class A fires wood, paper, textile etc.

**WARNING
DO NOT USE ON BURNING LIQUIDS
OR LIVE ELECTRICAL EQUIPMENT**

Use upright

Pull out red clip

Aim nozzle at base of fire

Squeeze handles

Recharge after complete or partial use
Protect from frost
F.O.C. approval ref. no. 758/22
Fire testing rating 13A

Model No. TG50

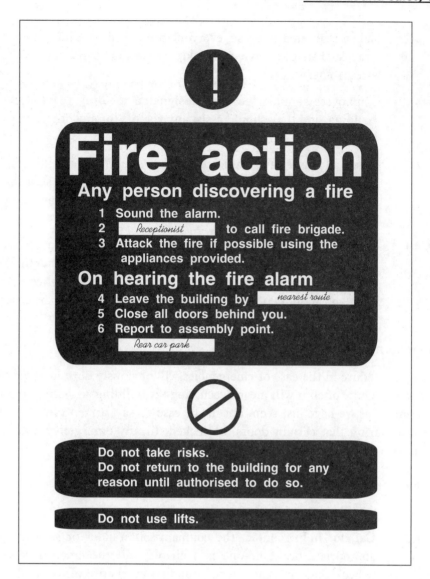

5 EMERGENCY PROCEDURES

Evacuation procedures

> **DEVOLVED ASSESSMENT ALERT**
>
> One of the potential sources of evidence of your competence in this Element is your being observed to take part in evacuation drills. Be aware of this: do not miss the opportunity! Do you know what to do in the event of an evacuation of your office? If not, make sure that you find out!

5.1 One of the most common reasons for evacuating staff from a building is the **outbreak of fire**. Other reasons include **bomb threats** and **unsafe buildings**.

5.2 Every organisation should have a set of procedures that should be followed when a building needs to be evacuated. Evacuations are generally conducted by a resident **safety officer** or **fire officer**. These officers usually have some sort of formal training by the local fire brigade or by the Health and Safety Executive, and are responsible for making sure that all persons known to be in a building at the time of evacuation can be accounted for.

BPP PUBLISHING

Step 1	When requested to do so, everyone present in a building that is to be evacuated should **leave as quickly as possible** using the quickest and safest route.
Step 2	Employees should meet at a **designated meeting place** outside the building, and they should assist any visitors (or any others who do not know where to go) to the correct meeting place.
Step 3	Once all staff have gathered at their relevant meeting place, the appointed fire officer or safety officer accounts for the staff that he is responsible for by calling a **register**. (This register is picked up as he is leaving the building.)
Step 4	Each employee must make sure that he or she is familiar with the organisation's **evacuation procedures** and **official meeting place**. Each office or department should clearly display notices detailing what you should do when the building you work in is to be evacuated.

Other emergencies

5.3 Safety procedure in the case of emergencies will obviously depend upon what has happened. Quite often it will mean evacuating the building according to fire safety procedures as we have just seen, but in the case of, say, armed intruders it might mean ensuring that certain doors are locked. In **any emergency situation** you should do the following.

Step 1	**Stay calm**.
Step 2	**Avoid personal danger**.
Step 3	**Call for help**: contact the company's first-aider or security staff as appropriate or, if no-one is available, call the emergency services. (Check that you know who your first-aider, fire officer and security officer are, and how to contact each of them.)
Step 4	**Help others** to avoid danger if possible.
Step 5	In no circumstances move injured people unless it is more dangerous not to do so. **Remove the source of danger** instead, if possible.
Step 6	**Do not attempt to administer first-aid yourself** unless you are trained to do so.

Calling the emergency services

5.4 In the UK you can be put straight through to the **police**, the **fire brigade** or the nearest **ambulance station** by dialling 999. The operators are very well trained and will guide you through the procedure.

Step 1	Once you are through you will be asked **which service** you require and be transferred as appropriate.
Step 2	Your call will be **traced automatically**, in case it is cut off for some reason: you will hear your telephone number being given to the person who will deal with your call. The call is also **tape recorded**.

Step 3   You will be asked for details of the **location** of the incident, what has happened, the number and approximate age of any casualties and the extent of the injuries, if any.

Step 4   **You should not hang up until after the person you are speaking to has done so** (otherwise he may not have all the information he needs).

Step 5   **If there is a casualty** try if possible to ensure that he or she is not left alone. Send somebody else to make the call but insist that they come back and tell you that the call has been made.

6   REPORTING PROCEDURES

Reporting potential hazards

6.1   In the case of illness, accident and fire at work, '**prevention is better than cure**'. Don't wait to display your competence in emergencies! If you are aware of a practice at work that is unsafe or if you think that conditions are unhealthy report it at once to your supervisor. You may be told that this is a matter for the personnel department, say, or a special safety officer, in which case report the matter to him or her.

6.2   When companies recognise trade unions, the trade union is allowed to appoint **safety representatives** chosen from the company's employees. If no action is taken after your initial approach and your employer has a safety representative, you should report the matter to him or her. Failing that you can get in touch with a Health and Safety Executive Inspector or the environmental health officer of the local authority. (The latter usually deals with offices; the former deals mainly with industrial premises.)

6.3   Contacting a third party is obviously a last resort: a well-run company will have a **proper reporting system and control procedures** to make sure that any potential hazards are reported and action taken to eliminate them. **Find out what the procedure is in your organisation.**

Reporting accidents

6.4   You may have an accident yourself, or you may witness one and be asked to make a **report**. No matter how minor an accident may seem at the time there may be complications later. The reporting procedure should ensure that the 'facts' are recorded accurately at the time for possible future reference. It should also alert those responsible to the need for extra safety measures.

6.5   Let us assume that you have had an accident. This is what you should do.

Step 1   Get **firstaid** (from someone properly **qualified** to give it)!

Step 2   **Report the incident as soon as possible** to someone in authority. You may be asked to fill in a form.

Step 3   If your company employs more than 10 people, it should by law keep an **accident book**. See that your accident is accurately recorded in the book – in other words read the entry for yourself if it is made by someone else.

BPP PUBLISHING

Step 4	If you are injured to the extent that you cannot immediately check the entry, **write to your employer** (or get somebody to write on your behalf) setting out your version of events.
Step 5	If anybody else witnessed the accident **get signed statements** from them and make sure that you know their names and addresses.

Obviously, again, not all of these measures will be necessary for a small cut or bruise, but you should be aware of the need to protect your own interests and those of other potential victims, in the case of a serious accident.

6.6   The drawing below shows the format of a **typical accident book**. The one used by your organisation may be laid out differently, or it might consist of loose-leaf sheets.

TO BE COMPLETED BY THE INJURED PARTY OR A WITNESS			TO BE COMPLETED BY FIRST AID OFFICER		TO BE COMPLETED BY SAFETY OFFICER
Date	Name	Details of accident (include time, place and names of any witnesses)	First aid treatment	Report to HSE	Preventative action taken

Notifiable accidents and diseases

6.7   **Certain accidents, dangerous occurrences** and **cases of disease** must be notified to:

- The **environmental health department** of the employer's local authority if the business is office based, retail or wholesale, warehousing, hotel and catering, sports or leisure, residential accommodation (excluding nursing homes) or concerned with places of worship

- The **Health and Safety Executive** for all other types of business.

6.8   The **Reporting of Injuries, Diseases and Dangerous Occurrences Regulations 1995 (RIDDOR 95)** require employers to do the following.

(a)   **Notify the enforcing authority immediately** (for example, by telephone) if:

- **There is an accident** connected with work and either an employee or self-employed person working on the premises is **killed** or **suffers a major injury** (including as a result of physical violence) or a member of the public is killed or taken to hospital.

- There is a **dangerous occurrence**.

(b) **Send a completed accident report form to:**

- **Confirm** within ten days a telephone report of an accident or dangerous occurrence as described in (a) above

- **Notify**, within ten days of the accident, any injury which stops someone doing their normal job for more than three days

- **Report** certain work-related diseases

6.9 **RIDDOR** contains a long list of what constitutes a **major injury**, a **dangerous occurrence** or a **notifiable disease**.

> ### KEY TERMS
>
> - **Reportable major injuries** include things like fracture 'other than to fingers, thumbs or toes', amputation, temporary or permanent loss of sight and any other injury which results in the person being admitted to hospital for more than 24 hours.
>
> - **Reportable dangerous occurrences** are 'near misses' that might well have caused major injuries. They include the collapse of a load bearing part of a lift, electrical short circuit or overload causing fire or explosion, the malfunction of breathing apparatus while in use or during testing immediately before use, and many others.
>
> - **Reportable diseases** include certain poisonings, occupational asthma, asbestosis, hepatitis and many others.

6.10 The **standard form** for the notification of injuries and dangerous occurrences is reproduced on the next two pages.

6.11 RIDDOR stipulates that if there is an accident, or if there is an incident which could have resulted in an accident, the incident or accident should be **investigated**. The site of the incident/accident should therefore be left undisturbed unless the site is dangerous to others and it is important that you are aware that you should not clear up what could be vital evidence.

BPP PUBLISHING

Health and Safety at Work etc Act 1974
The Reporting of Injuries, Diseases and Dangerous Occurrences Regulations 1995

Report of an injury or dangerous occurrence

Filling in this form
This form must be filled in by an employer or other responsible person.

Part A

About you

1 What is your full name?

2 What is your job title?

3 What is your telephone number?

About your organisation

4 What is the name of your organisation?

5 What is its address and postcode?

6 What type of work does your organisation do?

Part B

About the incident

1 On what date did the incident happen?

/   /

2 At what time did the incident happen?
(Please use the 24-hour clock eg 0600)

3 Did the incident happen at the above address?

Yes ☐   Go to question 4

No ☐   Where did the incident happen?

☐ elsewhere in your organisation - give the name, address and postcode

☐ at someone else's premises - give the name, address and postcode

☐ in a public place - give the details of where it happened

If you do not know the postcode, what is the name of the local authority?

4 In which department, or where on the premises, did the incident happen?

Part C

About the injured person

If you are reporting a dangerous occurrence, go to Part F.
If more than one person was injured in the same incident, please attach the details asked for in Part C and Part D for each injured person.

1 What is their full name?

2 What is their home address and postcode?

3 What is their home phone number?

4 How old are they?

5 Are they
☐ male?
☐ female?

6 What is their job title?

7 Was the injured person (tick only one box)

☐ one of your employees?

☐ on a training scheme? Give details:

☐ on work experience?

☐ employed by someone else? Give details of the employer:

☐ self-employed and at work?

☐ a member of the public?

Part D

About the injury

1 What was the injury? (eg fracture, laceration)

2 What part of the body was injured?

3 Was the injury (tick the one box that applies)

☐ a fatality?

☐ a major injury or condition? (see accompanying notes)

☐ an injury to an employee or self-employed person which prevented them doing their normal work for more than 3 days?

☐ an injury to a member of the public which meant they had to be taken from the scene of the accident to a hospital for treatment?

4 Did the injured person (tick all the boxes that apply)

☐ became unconscious?

☐ need resuscitation?

☐ remain in hospital for more than 24 hours?

☐ none of the above?

Part E

About the kind of accident
Please tick the one box that best describes what happened, then go to part G.

☐ Contact with moving machinery or material being machined

☐ Hit by a moving, flying or falling object

☐ Hit by a moving vehicle

☐ Hit by something fixed or stationary

☐ Injured while handling, lifting or carrying

☐ Slipped, tripped or fell on the same level

☐ Fell from a height
How high was the fall?

☐ _____ metres

☐ Trapped by something collapsing

☐ Drowned or asphyxiated

☐ Exposed to, or in contact with, a harmful substance

☐ Exposed to fire

☐ Exposed to an explosion

☐ Contact with electricity or an electrical discharge

☐ Injured by an animal

☐ Physically assaulted by a person

☐ Another kind of accident (describe it in part G)

Part F

Dangerous occurrences
Enter the number of the dangerous occurrence you are reporting. (The numbers are given in the Regulations and in the notes which accompany this form.)

☐ _____

Part G

Describing what happened
Give as much detail as you can. For instance
• the name of any substance involved
• the name and type of any machinery involved
• the events that led to the incident
• the part played by any people.
If it was a personal injury, give details of what the person was doing. Describe any action that has since been taken to prevent a similar incident. Use a separate piece of paper if you need to.

Part H

Your signature

_____

Date

☐ __ / __ / __

Where to send the form
Please send it to the Enforcing Authority for the place where it happened. If you do not know the Enforcing Authority, send it to the nearest HSE office.

For official use
Client number   Location number   Event number

☐ INV   REP ☐ Y ☐ N

BPP PUBLISHING

Activity 1.12

Look back at the scene from everyday office life in Activity 4.10.

Adopt the role of each of the three workers shown and, assuming that you have by now had one of the many accidents possible in this working environment, fill out a report in the Accident Book shown below.

Accident book

Full name, address and occupation of injured person (1)	Signature of injured person or other person making this entry* (2)	Date when entry made (3)	Date and time of accident (4)	Room/place in which accident happened (5)	Cause and nature of injury † (6)
1					
2					
3					
4					
5					
6					
7					
8					
9					
10					

* If the entry is made by some person acting on behalf of the employee, the address and occupation of that person must also be given

† State clearly the work or process being performed at the time of the accident

Key learning points

- When using **office equipment,** take care to ensure that operating instructions are followed carefully. As with equipment, **machinery** needs to be handled with care, especially those devices which are designed to puncture or cut things.

- The way in which an office is laid out is determined by economy of space, efficiency, security and also the **safety** of the employees. The **office layout** should also consider the movement of staff and the movement of documents (or **workflow**). Individual work areas and workstations should be organised in order to minimise hazards in the workplace.

- **General rules regarding fire safety**

  ○ There must be adequate means of escape

  ○ Doors out of the building must be able to be opened from the inside

  ○ Employees should be familiar with the fire alarm system

  ○ A fire alarm system must be present. It must be effective and regularly tested

  ○ Firefighting equipment must be easily available and in working order

- **General rules for dealing with emergencies**

  ○ Remain calm
  ○ Avoid personal danger
  ○ Call for help
  ○ Help others
  ○ Remove source of danger if possible
  ○ Administer first aid, only if you are trained to do so
  ○ Only move injured people if it is less dangerous to do so

- If you have an **accident** at work, here is what you should do.

  ○ Get first aid

  ○ Report the incident as soon as possible to someone in authority

  ○ Make sure your accident is recorded accurately in an accident book

  ○ Get the names and addresses of any witnesses and get signed statements from them

Quick quiz

1 What Is Repetitive Strain Injury?

2 What are the main causes of fire in the workplace?

3 What are the main types of fire equipment and facilities maintained by employers?

4 What are the main reasons for evacuating a building?

5 Outline the steps involved in calling the emergency services.

6 What should you do if you have an accident at work?

7 What is 'RIDDOR'?

Answers to quick quiz

1 A condition that arises when you work for long periods at a VDU. Common complaints include back ache, eye strain and muscular problems.

2 Smoking, flammable substances left in the wrong place, electrical applications.

3
- Fire doors
- Fire notices
- Fire alarms
- Fire extinguishers

4
- Fire
- Security alert (eg bomb scare)
- The building is deemed to be unsafe

5
- Dial 999 (in the UK)

- State the emergency service that you require

- Give details of the incident, location, what happened and details of any casualties (if any)

- Do not hang up until you are sure that the person you are speaking to has all of the information that he needs

6
- Get first-aid

- Report the accident as soon as possible

- Check to see that your accident is recorded correctly in your organisation's accident book (if there are less than ten employees then your organisation is not required by law to hold such a book)

- Get signed statements, and names and addresses from witnesses

7   The Reporting of Injuries, Diseases and Dangerous Occurrences Regulations (1995).

2 Security at work

This chapter contains

1   Introduction to security

2   Security risks

3   Security devices and procedures

4   Security of information

Learning objectives

On completion of this chapter you will be able to:

- Carry out organisational security procedures correctly

- Identify security risks correctly

- Put right, or report promptly to the appropropriate person, identified security risks

- Deal with identified breaches of security, in accordance with organisational procedures

- Outline the organisation's security and reporting procedures

- Understand your own scope and limitations in dealing with security risks

Performance criteria

(1)   Organisational security procedures are carried out correctly

(2)   Security risks are correctly identified

(3)   Identified security risks are put right or reported promptly at the appropriate person

(4)   Identified breaches of security are dealt with in accordance with organisational procedures

Range statement

1   **Security systems:** personal identification; entry; exit; equipment

BPP
PUBLISHING

1   INTRODUCTION TO SECURITY

1.1   It is difficult to pin down the meaning of the word **security**. Basically it is used in the sense of defending things against people or events which might take them away or harm them. Think of 'job security' or 'financial security', or feeling 'secure' amongst your family and friends.

> ### KEY TERM
>
> **Security** involves measures taken to protect against theft, espionage, unauthorised access and so on.

1.2   In the context of Unit 22, we are concerned with the **security of the workplace**: the building where you work and the people and physical things in it. The security of **information** is also very important - especially its **confidentiality** - but this will be discussed in more detail later in this Text.

The principles of security

1.3   Effective security is a combination of first **delay** and then **alarm**.

Step 1   **Delay** is achieved by having **several lines of defence before any vulnerable items can be reached.**

(1)   **Outer doors** to its main building

(2)   A **reception** area to greet guests but also to screen out unwanted intruders into the building.

(3)   **Further doors** guarding rooms where valuable items such as computers are kept

(4)   **Lockable drawers and cabinets** in which smaller items are kept

Step 2   **Raising the alarm**, once an intruder is identified, so that those responsible for dealing with the problem have time to get to the scene and take action.

(1)   **Electronic devices**
(2)   **Alertness and prompt actions**

2   SECURITY RISKS

At-risk items/people

2.1   Security aims to prevent others from taking away or doing damage to things that belong to your organisation or people that work for it. What type of belongings or people are particularly **at risk**? Here are ten suggestions. Try to think of more that apply in your organisation.

- Cash and cheques

- Stocks

- Vehicles

- Moveable equipment such as computers

- Confidential files and documents (on paper or floppy disk)

- Ownership documents like share certificates, title deeds and so on

- Pass cards allowing access to the building, or secure parts of it

- Staff in the front line (security guards)

- Staff with custody of assets (eg counter staff in banks)

- Key personnel, who may be held to ransom.

Vulnerable points in premises and procedures

2.2 What are the most **exposed or vulnerable** areas of an organisation? Again, here are some suggestions, but think what others might apply in your own organisation.

(a) **Public or open areas,** such as entrances, hallways, parking areas, toilets, stairways and lifts - especially if these are unattended, or inadequately attended for the volume of traffic.

(b) **Points of entry and exit** - such as doors, windows, gates and lifts. By definition, these are points where 'outsiders' may attempt to gain access.

(c) **Isolated areas,** such as store rooms or back stairs, where there are not always people about.

(d) **Ill-lit areas,** such as car-parks or stair wells.

(e) **Reception areas,** since if an unauthorised person can talk, trick or slip his way past reception, he may be much harder to identify as a stranger, and locate within the premises, later.

(f) **Areas where at-risk objects are concentrated,** such as store rooms, computer rooms, offices, file stores and so on - especially if they are located near points of entry or exit, or busy public areas.

(g) **Points of transit or storage** outside the organisation's premises. Valuable items taken out of the office (for banking, delivery, work at home or whatever) are particularly vulnerable.

DEVOLVED ASSESSMENT ALERT

The evidence requirements for Element 22.2 include the following. 'Evidence is ... required of identifying security risks.' Without being paranoid about it, keep an eye out at work (and in simulations) for the two elements of at-risk items/people and vulnerable points in premises and procedures.

Activity 2.1

What security risk(s) can you identify in the following, and what could be done in each case to minimise the risk?

(a) There is one person on the reception desk in a busy entrance area, and she is dealing with five impatient people trying to get visitors' tags and directions, plus two couriers trying to deliver packages.

(b) It is very hot in the office, so the back door (at the end of the corridor by the storerooms) has been propped open to allow air to circulate.

(c) A visitor has been shown into your supervisor's office and asked to wait: he is early for an appointment, and your supervisor has not yet returned from lunch. Nobody else knew about the appointment. The visitor says he does not wish to be in the way, and shuts the office door.

---

3 SECURITY DEVICES AND PROCEDURES

Security devices for controlling access

3.1 **Controlling access** will usually involve a combination of devices and procedures for:

- **Controlling people's ability physically to open points of access,** such as gates, doors and windows

- **Identifying people** as authorised or unauthorised individuals for entry to the premises or particular areas.

3.2 **Methods of controlling access to a building**

(a) **Doors can be closed and locked**. For particularly sensitive areas extra-strong doors can be used.

(b) **Windows can be closed and locked**. Sensitive areas may also have strengthened glass or even bars across the windows.

(c) **Plastic cards** (like cashpoint cards) that have to be inserted into a device at a door are used in some organisations.

(d) **Combination locks in the form of electronic keypads**. Only people who are authorised to enter a particular area are told the combination number. This number triggers off a switch which unlocks the door. The code can be changed from time to time.

(e) **Video cameras** may survey the entrance so that the person who is responsible for opening the door to visitors can see who is waiting outside.

(f) **Entryphone system** can require the caller's to state their business before being allowed in.

(g) **Voice recognition**. A computer controlling the door lock responds only to those voices recorded on its files. This method is far from common, however.

(h) In the future we are likely to see systems that recognise visitors' **fingerprints**.

3.3 **Cabinets, cupboards** and **drawers** can also be protected by means of locks. Some items should always be kept in a **safe,** cash being the most obvious example. The more valuable the item, the stronger the safe should be. Most have **keys** and **combinations**. Some have **electronically-controlled time-locks**.

Security procedures

3.4 Most organisations of any size have to have some **formal security measures,** if only to satisfy their **insurers**. The extent of the measures will depend on the risks involved in the business.

DEVOLVED ASSESSMENT ALERT

The evidence requirements for Element 22.2 include the following. 'Performance evidence ... must be available of the candidate **following set procedures** for the security of the workplace and its contents.' Such evidence may be as simple as being observed using passwords, signing in and out as required, locking cabinets and so on. Don't take these routine things for granted!

3.5 If your organisation has a formal **security procedures manual** get hold of a copy and read it carefully. It is likely to have the following procedures.

Procedure for	Examples
Identifying regular staff	If the procedures state that you should wear your **identity badge** at all times, then you must do so, no matter how well known you are to the security staff.
	If the procedures state that you should **show your pass** to the security guard whenever you enter the building, you should do so, and you should not be allowed access if you do not do so.
	Likewise if you are required to **sign in and out**, don't forget to do so.
Vetting non staff members	If somebody is coming to visit you on business then you may be required to go down to reception and accompany them to the place where you work. If you have not met them before you may have to ask them to produce some further means of identification: a letter inviting them to a meeting or the like.
Non business visitors	Say a friend is meeting you for lunch. Some organisations will not let such visitors past reception at all. Others allow free access to non-sensitive areas. Make sure your friend does not unwittingly break the rules.
Protecting the building	A particular door may have to be kept locked at all times. It may be the individual's responsibility to ensure that all windows in his or her working area are closed and locked at the end of the day.
Protecting the organisation's assets	You might be expected to lock away items like calculators in your desk drawer at night, for example.
Protecting documents and information	Locking away files and ledgers, or not leaving your computer terminal in a state where it can be used by someone without the password, are typical of measures of this sort. Other aspects of your work may be sensitive, and there may even be a confidentiality clause in your contract of employment: check.

Procedure for	Examples
Protecting the procedures	It ought to go without saying that you should not reveal your computer password to others and there is no point in having doors or safes with combinations if the combination is given to anyone who asks for it. Likewise there should be procedures to control keys – such as a list of authorised keyholders and instructions about where keys should be kept. There is no point in locking doors if the keys are accessible to all. In fact, do not discuss your organisation's security procedures with *anyone* outside the organisation: if an outsider asks persistently about security, report this as suspicious.
Explaining what to do in the event of a breach of security	The names and numbers should be available of the people to ring, and of the information they will need to be told: location of the intruders, time of entry, how many there are, items missing or damaged, and so on.

3.6   In general, your employer has **no right to search** employees or visitors **without their consent**. However, some contracts of employment include a clause giving the employer this right, in contexts where 'pilfering' of stock, components or files is a particular risk or problem.

3.7   The right to **search visitors** can be secured simply by displaying a notice informing them (before they enter the premises) that they are liable to be searched. (This is often the approach of retail outlets, to deter shoplifting.)

Activity 2.2

Choose any one area of security (personal identification, entry and exit, security equipment, data security, breach of security and so on) and design a notice or poster, suitable for posting on a departmental noticeboard, outlining the procedure **and/or** communicating its importance to staff.

(If your notice accurately and effectively communicates a real procedure or procedures in your office, consider seeking authorisation to post it on a noticeboard - and keep a copy for your portfolio.)

The scope and limitations of your responsibility

3.8   There will obviously be a limit to the responsibility that *you*, as an accounts assistant, have for the security of your organisation, its premises, belongings and staff. Find out exactly what your **responsibilities** are in this respect and where they stop. Most probably they will stop with your:

- **Following the rules** that affect your behaviour directly

- **Notifying the appropriate person** if you become aware of a security problem. (Who is the appropriate person in your organisation? Make sure you know.)

3.9   There is no need to report every person who stops in the street outside. Use your discretion, otherwise you will not be listened to when you do have a serious point to make.

3.10   **Tact** is very important. Some people can be offended if you question who they are: but most should understand that you are only doing your job.

3.11 **So what can you do to help?**

(a) If you see a door or cabinet gaping open and know that it should be locked, **lock it**.

(b) If you see anybody who is definitely acting suspiciously, **report it**.

(c) Make sure that **new recruits** to your department know what procedures they are supposed to follow.

(d) Don't allow **others** to allow you to breach security. Even if the person on reception knows you so well that he doesn't need to see your pass, there is no harm in showing it to him anyway. It reminds him of part of *his* job, and helps him to do it more effectively when strangers enter the building.

(e) Be aware that **things are changing** in your organisation all the time. A development that affects your work directly may not have been thought about by others from the security angle: a new procedure for handling cash, say, or moving the safe over to a desk by a ground floor window while the decorators are in.

(f) If you are going **out** to meet a client or supplier, make sure somebody in the office knows: where you are going, who *exactly* you are going to meet, what time you will be back and (if possible) a contact phone number. Be careful when meeting a new client or supplier for the first time off your premises; make sure your office knows exactly who the person is, where they come from, and what the purpose of the meeting is.

(g) **Don't be a hero**, if you find yourself in a dangerous situation. Your organisation can replace its belongings: **the safety of people comes first**.

DEVOLVED ASSESSMENT ALERT

The evidence requirements for Element 22.2 include "taking appropriate action (to deal with security risks) within the limits of your own authority". If you have keys to a filing cabinet, or the password to a computer, *you* are responsible for using them. If a stranger is acting suspiciously in the hallway, or is not wearing an identity card, what are you authorised to do? If in doubt, know exactly to whom you would *report* a suspected breach of security (or an actual breach, such as a theft).

Activity 2.3

In answering the following questions you should explain what your own organisation's security procedure is, if it covers the scenario described. If not, state what you think would be the best course or courses of action.

(a) A man with a case full of tools has opened up your office photocopier and spent about five minutes peering into it and tinkering with it. Nobody seems to know who called the engineer in, or whether there was a fault in any case.

Eventually the man tells you that the photocopier cannot be repaired on site and will have to be taken away. He calls in an assistant who has been waiting in a van outside and the two of them start to wheel the copier away You are the most senior person in your department at the moment because your boss is on holiday.

What should you do before you allow the men to take away the photocopier?

(b) Your security pass has the most appalling photograph of you that has ever been seen. You are meant to wear it on your lapel at all times but you are getting fed up with the jokes and comments about the 'accounts assistant from hell' and so on.

Given that you are well known to the security staff and to others in the organisation with whom you have to deal, is there any reason why you should not just keep your pass in your pocket?

(c) You are minding the reception desk and the telephone rings. A highly abusive person comes on the line and starts to make threats of physical violence against the MD of your company who is mentioned by name and accurate physical description.

What should you do?

(d) The chief cashier has an accident in the cashier's office, a secure part of the building to which no unauthorised access is allowed. You are the only other person present in the cashier's office. The chief cashier needs medical attention.

What should you do?

(e) You work in a small building society which keeps all of its mortgage documents in a strong room (the 'Deeds Room') in the basement. You are required to work in the Deeds Room for about two hours.

What security and safety issues arise here?

4 SECURITY OF INFORMATION

4.1 We will be discussing security of information, or **confidentiality,** in detail in Part C of this Interactive Text, when we deal with the storage and handling of information.

KEY TERM

Confidentiality is the keeping of information, given 'in confidence' to particular parties, between those parties; not disclosing information to those not authorised to have access to it.

4.2 **Information** is an item at risk of security breach. It can be damaged, lost or stolen in the same way that equipment and valuables can. People may seek to sabotage or steal information from organisations for

- Monetary/sale value
- Competitive advantage
- Pure nuisance value

4.3 **Organisations seek to protect the confidentiality of certain types of information**

(a) Information integral to the business's **standing and competitive advantage** - for example, unique product formulae, designs and prototypes, marketing plans and some financial information.

(b) **Personal and private i**nformation relating to employees and customers - for example, grievance, disciplinary and salary details; customer credit ratings. (Some such information is protected by law.)

(c) **Information related to the security of the organisation** - for example, details of access codes, computer passwords, banking/delivery schedules.

(d) Information **integral to the outcome of dealings,** which would be affected by public knowledge - for example, legal or financial details of intended mergers, takeovers, redundancies.

4.4 Extending the principles of premises security to 'sensitive' information, you should consider the following - and any special rules and procedures set by your organisation.

(a) Do not leave **paper files** or **computer disks** where they are generally accessible (preferably, lock them away).

(b) **Lock** secure safes, boxes and filing cabinets when you have finished with them.

(c) Use **passwords,** where advised, to secure computers and computer files.

(d) **Do not share passwords,** combinations or keys with unauthorised people.

(e) Do not copy, transmit or send confidential information without **authorisation** and appropriate security measures.

(f) Select **appropriate communication channels** and media for confidentiality. (There is a big difference between a memo posted on a staff noticeboard, or a conversation in an open office, and a sealed letter or memo clearly marked 'Private and Confidential' or 'For addressee's eyes only'!) **Remember that e-mail is neither secure nor confidential.**

(g) **Avoid 'careless talk' or gossip** about sensitive work-related matters with, or in the hearing of, unauthorised people. (This includes mobile phone conversations in public!)

(h) **Respect the privacy of others** - and assertively request them to respect yours.

Key learning points

- Security is a combination of **delaying** unauthorised access and sounding the **alarm** promptly when a breach of security has been identified.

- **Access** - entry and exit - points must be controlled, as **vulnerable areas** of any premises.

- Attention should be given to the protection of **people, confidential information** and the **assets and resources** of the organisation (including money, tools and equipment).

- A wide variety of **security devices and procedures** may be in place in a given organisation. These should be (a) clear to all employees involved and (b) regarded as confidential.

Quick quiz

1   List five items that might be at risk of being stolen from an office.

2   Outline a three-step procedure for identifying authorised staff at work.

3   What measures can help keep security procedures secure?

4   Give two examples of how another person could lead you into a breach of security.

5   List three ways of keeping information secure.

Answers to quick quiz

1   Cash, cheques, stock, vehicles, computers, fax machines, files (and so on).

2   Showing an entry pass to the security guard at reception; wearing an identity badge at all times; signing in and out of the building.

3   Don't reveal passwords or combinations. Control access to keys. Don't describe procedures to outsiders.

4   A guard or receptionist not requiring you to show your pass. Someone asking to borrow your keys for unspecified purposes.

5   Computer passwords. Locked file cabinets. Avoiding careless talk.

Answers to activities

Answers to Chapter 1 activities

Activity 1.1

(a)   At worst, a serious accident may render you **permanently unable to work**.

(b)   **You may be forced to stay away from work for a considerable period**. Employers generally allow a period of weeks or months on full pay, perhaps followed by a further period on half pay. The period is probably not as long as you think - check your contract of employment. Thereafter you will only receive state benefits.

(c)   Your career or training will be interrupted. You might miss a sitting of professional exams, putting you back six months!

Activity 1.2

You should have answered from your own workplace experience. Note that the issue of communication and awareness is crucial: the best safety policy in the world is no good unless people **know** about it!

Activity 1.3

(a)   Temperature. The temperature must be 'reasonable' inside buildings during working hours. This means not less than 16° C where people are sitting down, or 13° C if they move about to do their work.

(b)   Eating facilities must be provided unless the employees' workstations are suitable for rest or eating, as is normally the case for offices. You may have mentioned that surfaces should be kept clean.

(c)   Room dimensions. Each person should have at least 11 cubic metres of space, ignoring any parts of rooms more than 3.1 metres above the floor or with a headroom of less than 2.0 metres.

(d)   Lighting should be suitable and sufficient, and natural, if practicable. Windows should be clean and unobstructed.

(e)   Ventilation. Air should be fresh or purified.

(f)   Equipment. All equipment should be properly maintained. Special rules apply to certain items like VDUs.

(g)   Sanitary conveniences must be suitable and sufficient. This means that they should be properly ventilated and lit, properly cleaned and separate for men and women. 'Sufficient' means that undue delay is avoided!

Activity 1.4

(*Tutorial note*. The main purpose of this activity is to encourage you to read the operating instructions for items of equipment.)

Frederick should be fully reassured that the laser beam cannot escape from the machine because it has protective housings and external covers. Then the use of the machine should be demonstrated to him, and he should be encouraged to use it himself.

The information about radio interference and telecommunication systems need not really concern Frederick, except that it provides further evidence that the manufacturers take health and safety seriously.

The warning regarding ozone emissions should be heeded: Frederick should be able to see that the laser printers have been positioned appropriately, that the room is properly ventilated, and that multiple laser printers are not being used simultaneously.

Activity 1.5

Your answer to this activity - a realistic assessment of the health and safety of your work area, together with any suggestions for improvement you may have been able to make - would make good documentary evidence of your competence in this element. You may wish to reformat your answer as a report for assessment - and action! - purposes.

Activity 1.6

The following are the most likely work-related causes.

(a) Sitting at a desk/chair that is set at the wrong height for you. One or both should be adjusted if possible.

(b) Using equipment in such a way or in such a position that it is placing unnatural strain on your back. The equipment should be repositioned as appropriate.

(c) Lifting items when you are not accustomed to doing so, and lifting them incorrectly, taking the strain on your back rather than bending your knees and using your legs. You should learn how to lift heavy objects properly.

Of course, your backache may not be caused by your new job at all, and if none of the above apply you should consider whether any aspect of your life outside work is to blame (a new bed, a new sporting activity or the like.)

Activity 1.7

Rearranging the layout of the office might minimise people bumping into things (or each other), or making unnecessarily long journeys with heavy loads. The measures in paragraph 3.28 minimise the risk of eye strain (by providing natural light), back and muscular strain (by cutting down on lifting and carrying), and accidents (by avoiding some causes of stress and loss of concentration, and by keeping foods and liquids away from work and machinery where they might cause damage).

Activity 1.8

Another activity which required active research rather than theoretical knowledge: keep the notes of your findings as evidence of awareness!

Activity 1.9

Keep a careful note of:

(a) whom you asked for the information, and how; and
(b) the information gained.

Together, these may demonstrate not only your knowledge of stress control (an aspect of organisational health) but also your competence in 'asking the appropriate people for any information, advice and resources required'. (See Element 23.3.2.)

Activity 1.10

You should have spotted the following hazards

(a) Heavy object on high shelf
(b) Standing on swivel chair
(c) Lifting heavy object incorrectly
(d) Open drawers blocking passageway
(e) Trailing wires
(f) Electric bar fire
(g) Smouldering cigarette unattended
(h) Overfull waste bin
(i) Overloaded socket
(j) Carrying too many cups of hot liquid
(k) Dangerous invoice 'spike'

If you think you can see others, you are probably right.

Activity 1.11

See Answer 1.8 above.

Answer 1.12

Accident book

	Full name, address and occupation of injured person (1)	Signature of injured person or other person making this entry* (2)	Date when entry made (3)	Date and time of accident (4)	Room/place in which accident happened (5)	Cause and nature of injury † (6)
1	Constantine Larousse 14 North Street Islington (Office Junior)	C Larousse	14/8/98	10.30 14/8/98	Rm 74	Tripped over trailing wire & bruised knees and elbows whilst carrying cups of coffee for fellow workers
2						
3	Marcus Davis 17 Albert Sq. Acton London W3 (Accounting Technician)	M Davis	=	=	=	Attempted to prevent injury to Constantine. Suffered minor scalding to chest from hot
4						coffee and punctured hand on letter spiker. Obtained first aid
5						
6						
7	Percy Lal 247 East Street Finchley	M Davis (as above)	=	=	=	Percy was standing on a chair trying to put a box on the shelf. It appears that he was
8						alarmed by the above incident, banged his head on the shelf, dropped the box and fell off the
9						chair. He has been taken to hospital.
10						

* If the entry is made by some person acting on behalf of the employee, the address and occupation of that person must also be given

† State clearly the work or process being performed at the time of the accident

Answers to Chapter 2 activities

Activity 2.1

(a) The receptionist's attention is overloaded. It would be easy, in the general to-and-fro, for an unauthorised person to get past her into the offices without the appropriate checks and procedures - whether intentionally or unintentionally. It might also be a temptation to let the couriers deliver direct to the offices - again, a risk if they are unescorted and unlogged. To minimise the risk, reception should - permanently, or on a temporary 'at need' basis - be manned by extra personnel: a 'back-up' reception person might be kept 'on call'.

(b) It is surprisingly quick work to slip through an open door, gather a bag, or armful of valuable items, and slip out again! It can be done - swiftly - right under the nose of unwary occupants, and in this case, there is added risk since the door and storerooms are (i) close together and (ii) out of the way of office traffic. A further risk exists of the door being forgotten at the end of the day, if it is not usually left unlocked. The only way to minimise this risk is *not* to open the back door, or to allow it to be opened on a security chain or with a security gate or grill.

(c) The risk is that the visitor is not *bona fide* - nobody has checked - and has been left alone and unobserved in the office, where he has unchallenged access to anything left lying around. Ways of minimising such a risk include: vetting such visitors at reception and giving proof (such as a visitor's card) that this has taken place; requiring visitors to wait at reception or in other open areas until the visitee is available; people who are expecting visitors warning others in the office and describing/naming the visitor so they can cross-check the visitor's identity informally - especially if the visitee might not be available; having someone escort and stay with a visitor at all times, tactfully; and, as a last resort, ensuring that the door to the supervisor's office is kept open, and the visitor is visible to staff until the supervisor's return.

Activity 2.2

Your answer will obviously depend on your choice of topic, your organisation's specific procedures, and your imagination and communication style. You may have chosen to outline the steps in the procedure (**without** simply copying them from the Procedures Manual!), or you may have opted for a reminder/warning poster such as (at its simplest) the following.

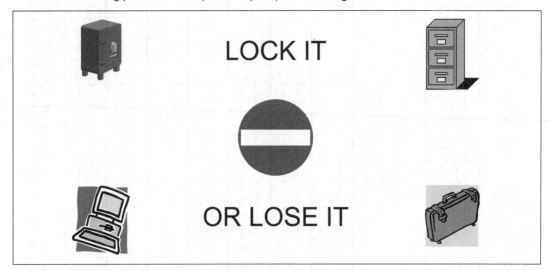

Activity 2.3

(a) The situation sounds very dubious: it is not usual for photocopiers to be repaired off-site. Here are some of the things that should be done.

   (i) Ask to see the men's identification.

   (ii) Under no circumstances allow them to take away the photocopier until you have established the facts. Get someone to keep an eye on them and make them a cup of tea. Don't let on that you are suspicious: say you are just going through the normal booking out procedures that have to be followed when assets are removed from the building and you'll get into trouble if you don't.

(iii)   Find out which company normally services the photocopier. Is this the company that the men claim to work for? You can start to be very suspicious if not.

(iv)   Telephone the company that the men claim to work for. Ask them to verify that the men do indeed work for them and they are responding to a call placed by someone in your organisation. Find out who in your organisation.

(v)   Telephone the person that called the men out and explain the situation. That person may then take responsibility for dealing with the situation.

(vi)   If the men do not work for the company they claim to work for, or if it does not exist, call the security department of your organisation, or the police if there is no security department. In fact if the men are thieves they would probably have made their escape by now, but you should still report the matter.

(b)   The reason is that your organisation *requires* all employees to *wear* their passes, and it is likely to have very strong grounds for doing so. Intruders will not stand out as people not wearing passes if bona fide personnel break the rules too.

If this matter is genuinely causing you distress, speak to your manager about it, or to another manager if your manager is one of the prime jokers. You could perhaps get another pass made up using your own, more presentable, photo, or at least get the issuer of passes to take a less unfortunate photo than the current one.

(c)   Simply see that the matter is reported at once to the MD. Assuming that you don't talk to the MD personally, make sure that the person to whom you give the message is reliable, and understands that you think the threats were serious. Your responsibility ends here, although the MD him or herself will probably want to check the facts with you directly, before taking further action.

(d)   If there is a telephone in the room notify firstly the first aid officer and secondly the security staff that help is needed and access for that help will have to be authorised. Stay with the injured person.

If you have to leave the room, leave it secure but accessible to authorised persons (ie don't run out leaving the keys locked inside!), get the help of the nearest available responsible member of staff and return to the injured person.

If it is left to you to authorise the entry of medical help when it arrives, make sure you see bona fide passes or documentation but don't cause undue delay.

(e)   Here are some of the issues. You may have thought of other matters.

(i)   The keys to the Deeds Room will probably be in the possession of certain nominated keyholders only. You will have to obtain the keys and perhaps have them booked out to you. The security of the Deeds Room will be your responsibility all the while the keys are in your possession.

(ii)   Procedures are likely to require the room to be kept locked at all times. You should not leave the door unlocked, even if you just have to pop out for a few moments.

(iii)   However, presumably (ii) means that the door should be kept locked while you are *inside*. This would be very dangerous, especially if the door were only able to be unlocked from the outside and there were no means of escape in an emergency. If this had not been thought about you ought to bring it to someone's notice. The Fire Service and your organisation's insurers would take a very dim view of this arrangement.

(iv)   No smoking rules will certainly apply. There may also be restrictions on food and drink.

(v)   There should be a telephone in the basement, in case of emergency.

(vi)   If someone else wants to enter the Deeds Room while you are inside and does not have their own key, you will need to be sure that they are who they say they are before you let them in.

(vii)   Would it not be better to do the work that you are required to do in your own office? Could the relevant files not be brought up to you?

(viii)   If (vii) is not possible, is the room properly equipped for the sort of work that you are going to do. Is there a desk and adequate lighting?

Practice Devolved Assessment

BPP
PUBLISHING

1 Practice devolved assessment Safe and Sound

Performance criteria

The following performance criteria are covered in this Devolved Assessment

Element 22.1 Monitor and maintain health and safety within the workplace

1   Existing or potential hazards are put right if authorised

2   Hazards outside own authority to put right are promptly and accurately reported to the appropriate person

3   Actions taken in dealing with emergencies conform to organisational requirements

4   Emergencies are reported and recorded accurately, completely and legibly in accordance with established procedures

5   Work practices are in accordance with organisational requirements

6   Working conditions which do not conform to organisational requirements are promptly and accurately reported to the appropriate person

7   Organising of own work area minimises risk to self and others

Element 22.2 Monitor and maintain the security of the workplace

1   Organisational security procedures are carried out correctly

2   Security risks are correctly identified

3   Identified security risks are put right or reported promptly to the appropriate person

4   Identified breaches of security are dealt with in accordance with organisational procedures

Notes on completing the Assessment

This Assessment is designed to test your ability to meet all of the performance criteria for Unit 22, as listed above.

You should attempt each of tasks 1 to 10. All the data needed is provided within each task.

You are allowed 3 hours to complete your work.

Correcting fluid may be used but should be used in moderation. Errors should be crossed out neatly and clearly. You should write in black ink not in pencil.

Do not turn to the suggested solution until you have completed all parts of the Assessment.

Task 1

What are your legal responsibilities as an employee with regard to health and safety at work?

Task 2

List as many ways as you can think of in which *you* can ensure that your working conditions are safe and secure.

Task 3

(a) You have to bind twenty copies of a report which are needed for a meeting that is due to start very shortly. Your boss points out to you that this can be done much more quickly if the binding machine is operated without the safety guard in place.

   What should you do?

(b) You are loading up a computer printer with paper and your hair (which is very long) gets caught in the machine. There is nobody else in the computer room.

   What should you do?

(c) You are visiting a client and you need to do some copying. There is only an ancient machine and you begin to feel light-headed, because it seems to give off fumes.

   What should you do?

(d) You are still at the client's, photocopying. The quality starts to get very poor and the machine indicates that it needs toner. You notice a packet on a nearby shelf and decide to top up the machine yourself, since you regularly do this on your own work premises. As you pick up the packet it splits open and your hands and arms are covered in toner.

   What should you do?

Task 4

Reproduced below are extracts from the General Guidance leaflet that should be contained in every first aid box. Read the extracts and then answer the questions that follow.

NOTE: TAKE CARE NOT TO BECOME A CASUALTY YOURSELF WHILE ADMINISTERING FIRST AID.

USE PROTECTIVE CLOTHING AND EQUIPMENT WHERE NECESSARY.

TREATMENT POSITION

Casualties should be seated or lying down when being treated, as appropriate.

Advice on treatment

If you need help send for it immediately. If an ambulance is needed, arrangements should be made for it to be directed to the scene without delay.

Priorities in first aid

(1)   BREATHING

[NOT SHOWN IN THIS EXTRACT]

(2)   UNCONSCIOUSNESS

[NOT SHOWN IN THIS EXTRACT]

(3)   SEVERE BLEEDING

Control by direct pressure (using fingers and thumb) on the bleeding point. Apply a dressing. Raising the bleeding limb (unless it is broken) will help reduce the flow of blood.

OTHER CONDITIONS

(4)   SUSPECTED BROKEN BONES

Do not move the casualty unless he is in a position which exposes him to immediate danger.

(5)   BURNS

BURNS AND SCALDS

Do not remove clothing sticking to the burns or scalds or burst blisters. If burns and scalds are small, flush with plenty of clean cool water before applying a sterilised dressing. If burns are large or deep, wash your hands, apply a dry sterile dressing and send to hospital.

CHEMICAL BURNS

Avoid contaminating yourself with the chemical.

Remove any contaminated clothing which is not stuck to the skin. Flush with plenty of clean, cool water for 10-15 minutes. Apply a sterilised dressing to exposed, damaged skin and send to hospital.

(6)   EYES

Loose foreign bodies in the eye: Wash out eye with clean, cool water.

Chemical in the eye: Wash out the open eye continuously with clean, cool water for 10-15 minutes.

People with eye injuries should be sent to hospital with the eye covered with an eye pad.

(7)   ELECTRIC SHOCK

Do not touch the casualty until the current is switched off. If the current cannot be switched off, stand on some dry insulating material and use a wooden or plastic implement to free the casualty from the electrical source. If breathing has stopped start mouth to mouth breathing and continue until casualty starts to breathe by himself or until professional help arrives.

(8) GASSING

Use suitable protective equipment.

Move casualty to fresh air.

If breathing has stopped, start mouth to mouth breathing and continue until casualty starts to breathe by himself or until professional help arrives. Send to hospital with a note of the gas involved.

(9) MINOR INJURIES

Casualties with minor injuries of a sort they would attend to themselves if at home may wash their hands and apply a small sterilised dressing from the first-aid box.

(10) RECORD KEEPING

An entry of each case dealt with must be made in the accident book.

(11) FIRST-AID MATERIALS

Articles used from the first-aid box should be replaced as soon as possible.

Tasks

(a)   You get a bit of grit in your eye. What should be done?

(b)   A courier falls down the main stairs just as lunchtime begins, when the traffic on the stairs is heaviest. She thinks she has broken her leg. What should be done?

(c)   A company's first aid box contains (amongst other things) a bottle of aspirin, a pair of nail scissors, a corkscrew, a ball of string, an 'eye pad', seven extra large wound dressings, some hand cream, a bottle of Optrex with an eye bath, a tube of Savlon and a bottle of TCP.

What should be done about this, if anything?

(d)   At the office Christmas Party the managing director inhales most of the contents of a helium-filled balloon and gives a speech in a squeaky voice. A minute or two later the managing director seems to be behaving and speaking quite normally. What should you do?

(e)   There is a small fire in your waste-paper bin and your shirt sleeve is burnt as you attempt (successfully) to put out the fire. What should you do?

(f)   You have just cut your finger at work and it is bleeding a little. This happened through your own carelessness and if you had done this at home you would just have ignored the wound and let the blood clot.

What should you do?

(g)   How should you free a casualty from an electrical source?

Task 5

Peter Spratt is a new manager in your department who started on Monday 3 April 19X6. He is very enthusiastic in everything that he does and rarely sits still. On his first afternoon he was striding past the kitchen as Helen Bruce emerged carrying two cups of coffee. Her right hand is still bandaged, because she was quite badly scalded.

The next day, fairly late in the morning, you heard a clatter and a muffled shout. About five minutes later Peter Spratt hopped into your office carrying a large bundle of rather battered looking files. He grimaced as he put his weight on both feet and seeing your concern he told you that he had just 'popped upstairs' and had 'had a bit of a spill'. You suggested calling the first-aid officer. He refused at first but you notice that his ankle is bandaged and that he is limping for the next few days.

By the following Thursday he appears to be fully recovered. As you were coming down the corridor that morning to do some photocopying you saw that he was crouching in front of the photocopier apparently trying to remove something. Rachel Preston was standing by holding a bundle of papers. There was a sudden flash and a loud noise and

Peter Spratt was slumped motionless against the opposite wall. You ran up, switched off the machine and pulled the plug from the wall. It seemed to be safe. You told Rachel to stand back but to remain with Peter Spratt while you got help. You phoned the first aid officer and then returned to the scene to await his arrival. You also phoned Mr Tompkins, the office manager and informed him that there appeared to be a problem with the photocopier. Your name is David Gardner.

Tasks

(a)   Complete the entries in your firm's accident book that would have been made by Helen Bruce, Peter Spratt, Rachel Preston and you. Use your imagination to supply any details that you have not yet been given.

(b)   Imagine that you are the firm's safety officer Xavier Dent. In the light of the above write a memo to all staff including any reminders that you think need to be made and indicating any action that will be taken.

(c)   Write the safety officer's entry or entries in the accident book.

Pages from the firm's accident book are shown on the following pages.

BPP PUBLISHING

TO BE COMPLETED BY FIRST AID OFFICER

TO BE COMPLETED BY SAFETY OFFICER

First aid treatment	Report to HSE	Preventative action taken

TO BE COMPLETED BY THE INJURED PARTY OR A WITNESS

Date	Name	Details of accident (include time, place and names of any witnesses)

	First aid treatment	Report to HSE	Preventative action taken
TO BE COMPLETED BY FIRST AID OFFICER		TO BE COMPLETED BY SAFETY OFFICER	

	Date	Name	Details of accident (include time, place and names of any witnesses)
TO BE COMPLETED BY THE INJURED PARTY OR A WITNESS			

	TO BE COMPLETED BY FIRST AID OFFICER		TO BE COMPLETED BY SAFETY OFFICER
First aid treatment	Report to HSE		Preventative action taken

TO BE COMPLETED BY THE INJURED PARTY OR A WITNESS		
Date	Name	Details of accident (include time, place and names of any witnesses)

Task 6

Now adopt the role of Peter Spratt. You want to set out your version of the photocopier accident and you decide to write a letter while you are recovering. You have often removed jammed paper from photocopiers before and you were familiar with this model. You woke up in hospital and knew nothing about the accident.

Write Peter Spratt's letter to his company, Duckley Ltd, Canardly Walk, London EC4A 9XJ. You may (for the purposes of this task) make up any further details that you feel are necessary.

Task 7

Knowing of your interest in health, safety and security matters, Xavier Dent has asked you to help with the investigation into the accident.

You are asked to complete as much of the form shown below as you can. If there are any details that you are unsure of write 'to be determined', but try to avoid this if you can. If you make any assumptions, note them in the comments column.

ACCIDENT INVESTIGATION QUESTIONNAIRE		
Name of injured person		
Date and time of accident		
Name of investigator		
Date of investigation		

Accident type

Exposure to explosion		Contact with electricity or electrical discharge	
Exposure to fire		Exposure to/contact with harmful substance	
Injured by animal		Contact with moving machinery	
Struck by vehicle		Injured while handling lifting or carrying	
Drowning or asphyxiation		Trapped by something collapsing or overturning	
Fall from height		Slip, trip or fall on same level	
Struck by moving object		Struck against something fixed or stationery	

Brief details of accident

Possible causes: please give, in order of importance, the code references of up to 5 possible causes (see the attached code sheet)

1 ....   2 ....   3 ....   4 ....   5 ....

BPP PUBLISHING

DETAILED ENQUIRY			
	YES	NO	COMMENTS
Was the person injured carrying out a task that was part of their normal duties?			
Was the person injured involved in an activity associated with work?			
Was the person's immediate supervisor present in the area at the time of the accident?			
If 'NO' state the location of the supervisor at the time and any specific instructions given by the supervisor prior to leaving the area.			
Was the accident reported immediately?			
If 'NO' state why there was a delay and how long the delay was.			
To whom was the accident reported?			
Has the task being performed been covered by a risk assessment?			
Was the injured person specifically warned of the hazards of the task?			
Was the person injured instructed to carry out the task?			
Was the task carried out in accordance with normal practice?			
Was the task within the capability of the person injured?			
Was the person injured familiar with the type of plant/equipment/tools etc?			
Had the person injured been trained to carry out the task safely?			

	YES	NO	COMMENTS
Was the task carried out by prescribed method?			
Was protective clothing being worn?			
Were any of the person's senses obscured/nullified which could have been a contributory factor?			
Were plant/equipment/premises in normal condition?			
Were guards/protective devices operating effectively?			
Were warning notices displayed warning persons of hazards or to use protective clothing?			
Was there a failure of service, component, plant or machinery?			
Is there a system for monitoring that procedures/instructions are followed?			

Did any of the following environmental factors contribute to the accident?

Rain	Snow	Ice	Fog	Cold
Humidity	Fumes	Gas	Vapour	Noise
Restricted space	Confined space	Uneven/unlevel surface	Condition of ground/floor	Radiation

BPP PUBLISHING

POSSIBLE CAUSES OF ACCIDENTS			
GENERAL		214	Personal protective equipment not provided or failed
000	No reasonably practicable precautions available	215	Weather conditions
ORGANISATIONAL FACTORS		216	Other (give details)
101	Inadequate training or instruction		EMPLOYEE OR OTHER PERSON'S CONTRIBUTION
101	Inadequate supervision	301	Loss of concentration
102	Inadequate standard of maintenance	302	Defeating safety devices
103	Inadequate traffic control system	303	Guarding device provided but not used
104	Other (give details)	304	Using obviously defective equipment
PHYSICAL FACTORS		305	Improper use of equipment including interference with equipment
201	Guarding devices failed	306	Failure to comply with or misinterpretation of instructions
202	Guarding devices inadequate	307	Failure to use available personal protective equipment
203	Guarding devices removed	308	Failure to give necessary warning to others
204	Electrical hardware fault (unearthed, uninsulated, overloaded, uncovered short, etc)	309	Recklessly going into hazardous situation
205	Instrumentation fault	310	Employee judgement error
206	Structural or physical aspects of premises	311	Assault
207	Poor housekeeping	312	Horseplay
208	Poor control of toxic substances	313	Working under the effect of alcohol or drugs
209	Poor control of flammable substances	314	Using unsafe or dangerous methods of handling or lifting
210	Inadequate standard of design	315	Riding or standing in an unsafe position
211	Inadequate standard of installation	316	Arson, burglary, vandalism
212	Illumination/heat/noise	317	Medical or physical condition of significance
213	Poor stacking or storage	318	Other

Task 8

'Health and safety is often seen as just being bureaucratic, and there is a reluctance to change familiar ways of working. There is also an element of male pride in being able to lift a heavy load. Many men do not like using equipment to move things when colleagues are not doing so. But employees have a responsibility for their own safety and are required to get a lifting aid if they need one.'

Safety Officer, DHL

Imagine that you are the junior member (male or female) of a team of staff that is about to visit a client's offices in Bristol on Monday for the following two weeks, travelling by train. Your organisation is based in central Manchester. You joined very recently and this is your first away job.

The deputy team leader tells you that the junior member has the honour of carrying the bulk of the files and papers needed for the job. Towards the end of Friday you are presented with two pilot cases (extra-large briefcases) and a carrier bag, all filled to capacity. You are told you should take them home with you at the weekend (you travel to work by public transport) and bring them with you to the station first thing on Monday morning.

You can lift the three bags, but they are very heavy. It is not going to be easy.

In the light of this scenario and the quotation preceding it, what practical options do you have and what are the likely consequences?

Task 9

According to Gee's *Essential Facts on Premises, Health and Safety*, there are three methods of protection from the consequences of a breach of security:

(a) defence;
(b) detection;
(c) deterrence.

Explain what you understand these three 'Ds' to involve for a typical organisation.

Task 10

At about a quarter to six one evening you are one of the few people left at work. You have stayed behind to take delivery of a package which is being sent over by courier from a client's building. You are waiting in the reception area.

The courier arrives, rings the buzzer in your entrance lobby and is admitted. He hands you the package, you sign for it and he leaves.

Less than a minute later the buzzer rings again. It is the courier, who tells you that his mountain bike has gone missing.

Apparently he had brought the bike through the main doors of your building and left it, unlocked, in the entrance lobby. There had been another person in the lobby who seemed to be tending to the plants by the door. The courier had left his bike unattended for no more than 30 seconds.

Your building is separate to the main building on your site where the security guards are located. You take the courier over to the main building and ask to speak to one of the guards to see whether they can shed any light on the matter. You also reassure the courier that the theft will have been captured on video since there is a camera overlooking the car park beside your building.

A new security shift begins at 6 o'clock and you find that you have to wait until then before you can speak to one of the guards. He tells you that, so far as he is aware, the theft had not been noticed and no suspicious characters had been reported.

Unfortunately the video had been switched off at 5.45 to rewind the tape, and had not been turned on again until just after 6 o'clock.

The security guard is reluctant to take any further action (he confides in you that he sees no reason to, since the courier is not a member of your organisation), but eventually you persuade him to let you watch the last few minutes of the tape that was switched off to see if you can at least spot the person who had been hovering in your entrance lobby. However it transpires that the camera points at the car park and any activity around the main entrance to your building cannot be seen.

Tasks

(a) Draw a diagram to illustrate the above scenario.

(b) Write a memo to the Office and Premises Administration Manager pointing out any aspects of security that you feel need to be tightened up.

Your name is Carol Hunter and the Office and Premises Administration Manager is called Eleanor Merton. You may embellish the scenario with any further details that you need to draw your diagram and write your memo or, if you like, you can substitute details that apply in the case of your own organisation.

2 Practice devolved assessment Portfolio

Performance criteria

The following performance criteria are covered in this Assignment

Element 22.1 Monitor and maintain health and safety within the workplace

1 Existing or potential hazards are put right if authorised

2 Hazards outside own authority to put right are promptly and accurately reported to the appropriate person

3 Actions taken in dealing with emergencies conform to organisational requirements

4 Emergencies are reported and recorded accurately, completely and legibly in accordance with established procedures

5 Work practices are in accordance with organisational requirements

6 Working conditions which do not conform to organisational requirements are promptly and accurately reported to the appropriate person

7 Organising of own work area minimises risk to self and others

Element 22.2 Monitor and maintain the security of the workplace

1 Organisational security procedures are carried out correctly

2 Security risks are correctly identified

3 Identified security risks are put right or reported promptly to the appropriate person

4 Identified breaches of security are dealt with in accordance with organisational procedures

---

Notes on completing the Assessment

This Assessment is designed to test your ability to meet all of the performance criteria for Unit 22, as listed above.

You should attempt each of tasks 1 to 13. All the data needed is provided within each task.

Tasks 1, 2, 3, 7 and 10 should be completed in the workplace and the evidence collected should be handed in to your tutor.

Spend no more than 2 hours completing the remaining tasks.

Correcting fluid may be used but should be used in moderation. Errors should be crossed out neatly and clearly. You should write in black ink, not in pencil.

Task 1

The Health and Safety Executive issue a guide entitled 'Five Steps to Risk Assessment'. This is mainly intended for employers but you can also use it to assess the risks to yourself in your work environment.

Complete the sections (adapted from the HSE guide) below. If you think you will need more room photocopy the pages and write on the back.

---

1   Look for the hazards

Look only for hazards which you could reasonably expect to result in significant harm under the conditions in your workplace. Here are some examples, but they are only a guide: other or different hazards may exist in your work environment.

Slipping/tripping hazards	Electricity
Fire	Dust
Chemicals	Fumes
Moving parts of machinery	Manual handling
Work at height	Noise
Ejection of material	Poor lighting
Pressure systems	Low temperature
Vehicles	

List hazards here

BPP PUBLISHING

2 Who might be harmed?

Health and safety is about thinking about others as well as yourself. There is no need to list individuals by name – just think about groups of people doing similar work or who may be affected, for example:

Office staff	Operators
Maintenance personnel	Cleaners
Contractors	Members of the public
People sharing your workplace	

Think especially about staff with disabilities, inexperienced staff, visitors and lone workers.

List groups of people who are especially at risk for the significant hazards which you have identified

3   Is the risk adequately controlled?

Have precautions already been taken against the risks from the hazards you listed? For example are you provided with adequate information, instruction and training? Do the precautions meet the standards set by a legal requirement, comply with a recognised industry standard, represent good practice and reduce risk as far as is reasonably practicable?

If so, then the risks are adequately controlled, but you need to indicate the precautions that are in place. Refer to procedures, manuals, company rules and so on giving this information.

List existing controls here or note where the information may be found

BPP PUBLISHING

4   What further action is necessary to control the risk?

What more could be done for those risks which you found were not adequately controlled?

You will need to give priority to those risks which affect large numbers of people and/or could result in serious harm. Apply the principles below when taking further action, if possible in the following order.

Remove the risk completely

Try a less risky option

Prevent access to the hazard (eg by guarding)

Organise work to reduce exposure to the hazard

Issue personal protective equipment

Provide welfare facilities (eg washing facilities for removal of contamination and first-aid)

List the risks which are not adequately controlled and the action you will take where it is reasonably practicable to do more. You are entitled to take cost (money, resources and time) into account, unless the risk is high.

5 Review the above assessment from time to time and revise it if necessary.

Task 2

(a) Draw a diagram showing the following.

    (i)   The layout of your office.

    (ii)   The route to the fire exit which you should use in an emergency.

    (iii)   The location of the nearest fire extinguishers, and the next nearest.

    (iv)   The location of the first aid box or cupboard.

(b) Annotate your diagram with the following information.

    (i)   The name, location and telephone number of the person responsible for first aid.

    (ii)   The name and number of the person to ring in case of emergency.

    (iii)   The location of your 'assembly point' in an emergency.

(c) Draw a bird's eye view of your own immediate work area - your desk and the area around it. Draw in any equipment that you keep on the desk and any cables that run up to it. Show your route to any filing cabinets or items of office equipment that you use regularly.

Mark on your drawing any potential hazards in your work area.

(d) Obtain the instruction manuals for all items of equipment that you use regularly and look through them for safety instructions. (These may come under headings like 'Warning', or 'Do's and Don'ts' or 'Fault finding', since manufacturers often reluctant to admit that their goods might be unsafe. Obtain copies of the relevant pages and include them in your portfolio.

(e) Collect as much of the following as you can. Tick the box when you are satisfied that you have the evidence.

    (i)   Details of hazards or emergencies that you have identified at work (tick if
you have completed Task 1).   ☐

    (ii)   Copies of any reports that you have made about these hazards, emergencies
or accidents.   ☐

    (iii)   Details of any hazards at work that you have put right.   ☐

    (iv)   A note of when you last took part in a fire drill or other evacuation
procedure, and what you were required to do.   ☐

    (v)   A copy of the relevant pages of your organisation's procedures manual (or similar) that explain the health and safety procedures to be followed. You should highlight those points that set out your responsibilities with regard to identifying, reporting and putting right hazards, and dealing with accidents and emergencies.   ☐

Task 3

Collect as much of the following information as you can. Tick the box when you are satisfied that you have the evidence.

(a)   Make a list giving details of all the security procedures that you are personally responsible for at work - ensuring that equipment is secure, locking your desk drawer, keeping the keys to a filing cabinet, or whatever.

(b)   Obtain a copy of any official manual that exists in your organisation detailing security procedures that affect your work (this will include things like showing passes, obtaining entry to secure areas and so on).

(c)   Prepare a record of any security risks in your organisation that that you have identified and/or dealt with in some way. This should include a description of the incident and copies of any reports or memos that you may have written.

(d)   Prepare a record of any breaches of security that you have dealt with. Again include a description and copies of any appropriate original documents.

Task 4

What, in your own opinion and experience, are the main health, safety and security risks facing staff who work in an *accounts* department (in other words, how risky is it to be an accountant rather than, say, a production worker)?

Task 5

You are a sales ledger assistant and most of your day is spent using a computer. Describe what *you* can do to make your workstation a safe and healthy working environment.

Task 6

What goes on in your head at work is at least as important as what goes on in or happens to your body. Psychological pressures are probably the biggest dangers faced by accountants.

The following paragraphs are adapted from the Health and Safety Executive's leaflet on Mental Health at Work.

> The workplace can be a stimulating and supportive environment and have a positive effect on mental health, but adverse situations can have a negative effect. Thus there is a great value in employers instituting an effective occupational health policy which routinely includes consideration of mental health aspects. Apart from reduction in personal distress for individuals, an effective policy will have positive benefits for the whole organisation.
>
> It has been estimated that 30-40% of all sickness absence from work is attributable to some form of mental or emotional disturbance. Organisational factors such as change, the design of the workplace, and approaches to management play a part. Some of the main *individual* work and domestic factors are as follows.
>
> (a)   Over promotion or resentment at failure to be promoted
> (b)   Too much or too little work
> (c)   Relocation, change in work environment or of colleagues
> (d)   Change in the nature of work or style of management
> (e)   Role conflict or ambiguity (not knowing what is expected of you or how you fit in)
> (f)   Irregular or long hours
> (g)   Lack of autonomy (not being able to decide for yourself how best to do a job)
> (h)   Family illness or bereavement
> (i)   Marital or family problems
> (j)   Financial difficulties
> (k)   Moving house
> (l)   Injury or illness which interferes with the quality of life.

People do not always, or even usually, realise that they have a problem. Early signs may include a sense of apprehension, sleep disturbance, impaired concentration and short term memory, change in appetite, lack of energy, indecisiveness or irritability. More severe signs may include spontaneous weeping, a sense of hopelessness or excessive alcohol or drug consumption.

Feelings of inability to cope and physical symptoms may occasionally prompt the seeking of assistance before anyone else realises there is a problem. Alternatively colleagues or supervisors may notice changes in patterns of behaviour such as:

(a) unusual irritability, resentment of advice and constructive criticism;
(b) becoming withdrawn and unsociable;
(c) unusual absenteeism or poor timekeeeping;
(d) overworking and failure to delegate;
(e) impaired performance;
(f) changes in appetite, personal appearance, habits and behaviour;
(g) increasing use of coffee, cigarettes, alcohol and drugs;
(h) accident proneness;
(i) unexpected difficulty with training and examinations.

You would be unusual if you have not suffered from some of these symptoms and problems yourself at some time.

Try to think back to a difficult period and describe (not necessarily in this order):

(a)   the circumstances that you think caused your problems;
(b)   how your work was affected;
(c)   how your colleagues were affected, if at all;
(d)   how the problem was solved;
(e)   what you feel your organisation should have done in the circumstances;
(f)   what your own responsibilities were.

Task 7

You can find out the answers to the following questions by inspecting a first-aid box. Ask permission before you do this and wash your hands first. Inspect it in its usual location – don't walk off with it for hours – and take care not to damage or tamper with the contents.

(a)   What are the standard minimum contents of a first-aid box?

(b)   What does the box that you are inspecting actually contain? Does it conform to the minimum requirements. Does it breach the requirements in any way.

(c)   What action should you take in the light of your answer to (b)?

Task 8

According to a recent crime survey there are 35,000 incidents of workplace violence every year, three-quarters of which are assaults on staff by members of the public.

If you were in a position that regularly required you to deal with members of the public in situations that could potentially become unpleasant, what would you do to protect yourself and what would you expect your employer to do?

Concentrate on *interview* situations (for example working in a benefit office), not situations that are prone to crime of other sorts such as (armed) robbery.

Task 9

What are the implications of the following?

A. N Employee

CONTRACT OF EMPLOYMENT (extracts)

During the period of your employment with the company and thereafter you shall keep secret the affairs of the company. At the termination of your employment for whatever reason you shall surrender to the company all files, records, documents and information belonging to or in the possession of the company in whatever form which shall include all electronically recorded information.

...

During the period of your employment the company reserves the right to conduct a search of your person and your personal belongings on your departure from the company's premises and in your presence any place on the company's premises where you may keep personal possessions. The search shall be undertaken by trained staff of the same sex.

NOTICE

DUE TO THE NATURE OF THE COMPANY'S ACTIVITIES, THE COMPANY RESERVES THE RIGHT TO SEARCH EMPLOYEES AND VISITORS ON DEPARTURE FROM THE PREMISES.

IF YOU ARE NOT PREPARED TO BE SEARCHED,

DO NOT

ENTER THE PREMISES

Searches are conducted by members of the same sex who are fully trained in search procedures.

Task 10

Read the article from a magazine reproduced below, and then carry out the tasks listed afterwards.

Caffeine may be a significant factor in work-related stress. It raises the levels of two of the key stress hormones, adrenaline and cortisol. People drink it for its initial 'pick-me-up" qualities but it has after effects such as lower blood sugar levels, which in turn lead to an inability to concentrate, poor decision making, irritability, nervousness, forgetfulness and fatigue, (these are the same symptoms that make people drink caffeine in the first place!)

Caffeine also accentuates the symptoms of pre-menstrual syndrome, causes diarrhoea and brings on insomnia.

Coffee contains the highest amount of caffeine (between 80 to 300 milligrammes per cup, depending on the type of coffee); tea contains between 50 and 100 milligrammes per cup; cola between 43 and 65 milligrammes per can. A large bar of chocolate can contain 60 milligrammes. It is reckoned to be wise to limit caffeine intake to between 200 and 250 milligrammes per day.

Tea was recently the subject of an international conference. The tea plant is rich in a chemical found in fruits and vegetables called polyphenols, that may help prevent heart disease and cancer. Research in the Netherlands, for example, has shown that men whose diets are richest in polyphenols have the lowest risk of having a heart attack. These men got 61% of their polyphenols from black tea. Similarly Japanese who drink more than 10 cups of green tea a day have lower rates of stomach cancer and of lung cancer (despite being heavy smokers).

(a) Based on the above article and any personal views or knowledge you may have, draw up a notice that could be put up in the kitchen or by the drinks machine at work to encourage better liquid refreshment habits.

(b) Keep a 'caffeine diary' for yourself for a typical week. You should note down how many cups of tea or coffee, cans of cola and bars of chocolate you have each day (both at home and at work) and then work out your daily average.

(c) If you can, encourage some of your colleagues at work to do exercise (b) at the same time as you.

(d) If you or your colleagues think you are exceeding the recommended maximum daily intake of caffeine, try reducing your consumption for a few days. Do you notice any benefits?

Task 11

Some organisations run incentive schemes to encourage safety in the workplace, for example having a prize draw when so many weeks of accident-free work have been achieved.

Devise such a scheme for your own workplace. Your scheme should include the following elements.

(a) Safety 'targets' to be aimed at.
(b) Incentives to encourage *all* workers to participate.
(c) Rules about what would give rise to incentives not being awarded.

Task 12

The three documents shown below were received by your company. What should be done in response to them?

BPP PUBLISHING

Cinders Fire Protection Ltd

CFP

Certificate of Inspection

Customer address

Khan & Co

Jemimah Road

Stevenage

Herts

Date ___14/1/X2___

Contract No. _____

Serviced		Recharge/Spares	12084
Fire/Intruder Alarm		Supplied: - 41 × Security tags	
Emergency Lighting		5 × Series 2000 clips	
Fire Protection System		6 × 0 Rings	
Water Extinguisher	26	Water extinguisher on 5th floor rear stairs condemned - corroded base (unfit for service last visit)	
Carbon Dioxide	6		
Dry Powder			
Foam		Recharged on site:-	
Hose Reels	8	1 × 9 litre water 6th floor main stairs	
B.C.F.	5	1 × 9 litre water ground floor end building (Breton House)	
F/Blankets			
Misc.			
TOTAL	45		

Recommendations:- Replace condemned water extinguisher on 5th floor rear stairs.

Serviced in Accordance with BS 5306: Part 3: 1985

Routine inspection by the user.

It is recommended that regular inspection of all extinguishers, spare gas cartridges and replacement charges should be carried out by the user or the user's representative at intervals, to make sure that appliances are in their proper position and have not been discharged, or lost pressure.
The frequency of inspection should not be less than quarterly, and preferably at least monthly.

Engineer's Signature ___Joe Bloggs___   **Customer's Signature** ___I Khan___

Cinders Fire Protection Ltd

CFP

SITE REPORT   51935

Site Address
Khan & Co
Jemimah Road
Stevenage
Herts

Customer address

SERVICE ☑	INSTALLATION ☐	CALLOUT ☐

	DATE	13/4/X6
QUARTERLY ☐	ARRIVAL TIME	7.20
6 MONTHLY ☑	DEPART TIME	
ANNUAL ☐	TRAVEL	
	TOTAL	

TYPE OF SYSTEM	
FIRE ALARM SYSTEM	☑
HALON SYSTEM	☐
INTRUDER ALARM	☐
DOOR ACCESS	☐
EMERGENCY LIGHTING	☑
OTHER	☐

REMARKS:- Tested and serviced fire alarm and emergency lighting. Fire alarm was found to be in good working order but found two emergency lights faulty : 5th floor rear room, 4th floor front lobby.

All servicing carried out in accordance with British Standard regulations.

PARTS USED:- Have replaced main ground floor supply fuse 60a MBC as when switching main switch, parts of an old fuse board left inside main switch shorted out. Main supply cupboard is in a poor state of repair.

	TYPE	TESTED
CALLPOINTS	KAC	✓
IONISATION	APPOLLO	✓
OPTICAL		
HEAT	" "	✓
SOUNDERS	BELLS	✓

CONTROL TYPE	
NO. OF ZONES	
UNITS TESTED AND OPERATING CORRECTLY	

ALL WORK COMPLETED	☐
FURTHER VISIT REQUIRED	☑

Engineer's Signature _Joe Bloggs_   **Customer's Signature** _I Khan_

Cinders Fire Protection Ltd

SITE REPORT   55366   CFP

Site Address	**Customer address**
Khan & Co	
Jemimah Road	
Stevenage	
Herts	

SERVICE ☑	INSTALLATION ☐	CALLOUT ☐

	DATE	14/11/X7
QUARTERLY ☐	ARRIVAL TIME	8.00
6 MONTHLY ☑	DEPART TIME	10.15
ANNUAL ☐	TRAVEL	

TYPE OF SYSTEM	
FIRE ALARM SYSTEM	☑
HALON SYSTEM	☐
INTRUDER ALARM	☐
DOOR ACCESS	☐
EMERGENCY LIGHTING	☑
OTHER	☐

REMARKS:- Serviced fire alarm and emergency lighting. All fire alarm tests OK. Emergency lights on 7th floor reception stairwell not working due to no mains supply.

All servicing carried out in accordance with British Standard regulations.

PARTS USED:-

	TYPE	TESTED
CALLPOINTS	KAC	20 ✓
IONISATION	APPOLLO	2 ✓
OPTICAL		
HEAT	APPOLLO	1 ✓
SOUNDERS		
MISC	E/L	28 ✓

CONTROL TYPE	Unknown
NO. OF ZONES	8
UNITS TESTED AND OPERATING CORRECTLY	

ALL WORK COMPLETED	☑
FURTHER VISIT REQUIRED	☐

Engineer's Signature _Joe Bloggs_   **Customer's Signature** _I Khan_

Task 13

What should you do if you see a machine with the following notice attached?

Downstown Local Authority
Town Hall
Rossney Road
Downstown
Keithshire KT23 2WE

PROHIBITION NOTICE

Health and Safety at Work etc Act 1974, sections 22, 23 and 24

To _____ *Mr J West*

_____ *14 Back Street*

_____ *Downstown*

Trading as _____ *D G Practices Ltd*

?._____ *Firmin Limpar*

one of _____ *The Environmental Health Officers*

of the Environmental Health Department, Town Hall, Rossney Road, Downstown
hereby give you notice that I am of the opinion that the following activities, namely

_____ *The operation of a paper shredding machine*

which are ~~being carried on by you/about to be carried on by you~~/under your control at

D G Practices Ltd

Back Street

Downstown

involve or will involve a risk/ ~~an imminent risk~~, of serious personal injury. I am further of
the opinion that the said matters involve contraventions of the following statutory
provisions:

The Provision & Use of Work Equipment Regulations 1992

Regulation 11 – Dangerous parts of machinery

Regulation 16 – Emergency stop controls

because *the operator of the machine is able to touch dangerous moving*

parts while the machine is working and the emergency stop control is not

functioning

and I hereby direct that the said activities shall not be carried on by you or under your
control immediately/ ~~after~~
unless the said contraventions in the schedule, which forms part of this notice, have
been remedied.

Signature *F Limpar*   Date *2 February 1998*

Being an inspector appointed by an instrument in writing made pursuant to Section 19
of the said Act and entitled to issue this notice.

BPP
PUBLISHING

Solutions to Practice Devolved Assessments

SOLUTION TO PRACTICE DEVOLVED ASSESSMENT 1: SAFE AND SOUND

Task 1

You have a general legal (and moral) duty to behave like a responsible person (not harm people, not set light to buildings and so on). Under the Health and Safety at Work Act 1974 you are obliged to do the following.

(a) Take reasonable care to avoid injury to yourself and others.

(b) Co-operate with your employers to help them comply with their statutory obligations.

Under the Management of Health and Safety at Work Regulations 1992 you have further responsibilities.

(a) You must use all equipment, safety devices, etc, provided by the employer properly and in accordance with the instructions and training received.

(b) You must inform your employer, or another employee with specific responsibility for health and safety, of any perceived shortcoming in safety arrangements or any serious and immediate dangers to health and safety.

Task 2

Here are some suggestions. You probably have others.

(a) Use equipment properly (don't attempt to do things like repairs unless you are properly trained to do so)

(b) Don't tamper recklessly with the electrical supply to equipment.

(c) Take care with inflammables and toxic things like aerosols and chemicals.

(d) Don't put liquids on or near equipment. Clean up spilled liquids immediately.

(e) Be careful with things designed to cut or puncture paper.

(f) Don't wear clothes or jewellery that are likely to lead to accidents: things that dangle are the worst!

(g) Follow the guidelines for working with VDUs: *adjust* your adjustable chair, use the blinds, take breaks and so on.

(h) Take care when moving about: look where you are going, be aware that there may be someone on the other side of the door or just round the corner.

(i) Make sure that your own work area is free of hazards such as obstructions that people could trip over, open drawers, hidden sharp implements, dangerous or unhygienic rubbish and so on.

(j) If you smoke don't cause fires: don't throw lighted cigarettes or matches into rubbish bins.

(k) Don't get intoxicated during working hours.

(l) Store things safely: heavy objects low down, lighter ones higher up. Don't stand on chairs that have wheels to reach high objects: use proper steps.

(m) Take care when lifting things: don't try to lift more than you can manage; bend at the knees and so on.

(n) Lock up things that are meant to be kept locked up.

(o) Carry and show your identification as required. Don't lend it to anyone else.

(p) Don't reveal passwords or combinations to unauthorised people.

(q) Follow organisational procedures for health safety and security.

(r) Report hazards and breaches of security promptly.

Task 3

(a)   You may have said that in practice you would have used the machine without the safety guard to avoid earning the disapproval or ridicule of your boss. If so, we hope you would be very careful. The only correct answer is that you would not compromise your own well-being by operating the machine unsafely and your boss should not expect you to do so.

(b)   The first thing you should do is switch off the printer at the wall if possible, but if you cannot reach then at least turn off the switch on the machine. You can then make tentative attempts to free yourself but you should not risk damaging yourself or the machine, so be gentle. If this fails, get help. If there is a telephone at hand, use that. Otherwise, you may have to shout for help or even wait for somebody to come. You may, unfortunately, have to cut your hair if it cannot be freed.

One thing that you may have forgotten is to *report* the accident: others should be warned to tie their hair back if they are carrying out the same task and/or the machine should be adapted so that this cannot happen again.

(c)   Leave the room for a while and get some fresh air. When you feel better go back and open a window if possible to make sure that there is proper ventilation. Finally be sure to point the matter out to whoever is responsible for the photocopier - it may have a fault. If you don't start feeling better, see the first-aid officer.

(d)   In the first place you should not have attempted do-it-yourself maintenance on a machine that is not familiar and not your responsibility. Given that you did, however, you should now do the following.

(i)   Read (what is left of) the packet: it should give instructions telling you what to do if the contents come into contact with your skin.

(ii)   Follow the instructions and remove the chemical immediately.

(iii)   Report the matter to whoever is responsible for the machine, even though you may feel guilty for interfering. They should see to it that the mess is cleared up immediately.

Task 4

This is an easy task because you are given all the answers. The purpose is to make you read the leaflet.

In general, any accident should be noted in the accident book.

(a)   Wash out your eye with clean, cool water.

(b)   Do not move the courier. Find some way of ensuring that people using the stairs have to go around the casualty (perhaps by blocking off one half of the stairs) or that they go another way entirely.

(c)   The only items on this list that are part of the standard minimum contents are the eye pad and the extra large wound dressings. All of the others should be removed. Report the matter to the person in charge of the box.

Individuals can, of course, carry aspirin, hand cream and so on around with them or keep them in their desk drawer, but they should not be administered to others as first aid.

(d)   Nothing, but don't try this yourself. If the MD later seems to be having breathing difficulties he should be moved to the fresh air until he is better or until professional help arrives.

(e)   If *you* are burnt (and not just your clothing) be careful not to remove clothing sticking to the burns, flush with plenty of clean cool water if the burns are small and then apply a sterilised dressing. If burns are large or deep, wash your hands, apply a dry sterile dressing and go to hospital.

(f)   You should wash the wound. Then do what you would do at home: either ignore it or put a plaster on it if it merits it. Health and safety at work is important, but don't get things out of proportion.

(g)   Turn off the current. If you can't do this stand on some dry insulating material and use a wooden or plastic implement.

Task 5

(a)

TO BE COMPLETED BY THE INJURED PARTY OR A WITNESS			TO BE COMPLETED BY FIRST AID OFFICER	TO BE COMPLETED BY SAFETY OFFICER	
Date	Name	Details of accident (incluce time, place and names of any witnesses)	First aid treatment	Report to HSE	Preventative action taken
3.4.X6	H. Bruce	3.20pm on 3rd floor kitchen. Spilt boiling coffee on right hand. Knocked into by Mr Spratt who was walking past. Witness: Mr Spratt			Isolated incident - no action taken
4.4.X6	P. Spratt	Twisted ankle running upstairs at about 11am - dropped files, attempted to catch them and fell headlong. No witness. On 4th floor landing.			I spoke informally to Mr Spratt who is hobbling and now realises the danger of running about the building.
13.4.X6	David Gardner (Witness)	10.47am. 3rd floor corridor by photocopier. Mr Spratt had his hand in the body of the photocopier and was red-faced because he was trying to pull something out. There was a flash and a loud bang and Mr Spratt was thrown backwards. I switched off the photocopier and phoned the First Aid Officer. Rachael Preston remained with Mr Spratt while I did so.			Memo issued to all staff re running and interfering with equipment. Safety lectures arranged for all staff.

	TO BE COMPLETED BY FIRST AID OFFICER		TO BE COMPLETED BY SAFETY OFFICER
	First aid treatment	Report to HSE	Preventative action taken

TO BE COMPLETED BY THE INJURED PARTY OR A WITNESS

Date	Name	Details of accident (include time, place and names of any witnesses)
13.4.X6	R. Preston (Witness)	10.40. 3rd floor. The photocopier jammed while I was using it. Mr Spratt came running past and I asked him for help. He pressed a few buttons and then opened the machine and started feeling about for the jammed paper. He thought he had found it and tugged but there was a loud bang and a flash and he fell backwards. He seemed to be unconscious, I stayed with Mr Spratt while Mr Gardner called the First Aid Officer. I did not touch him or move him, and he did not speak or move. I left when the First Aid Officer arrived.

(b)

MEMORANDUM

To: All staff   Date: 14 April 20X6

From: Xavier Dent, Safety Officer

Subject: Safety in the workplace

No doubt you have all heard about the accident to Mr Spratt on the 3rd floor last Thursday.

I am glad to report that Mr Spratt is now resting at home and is not seriously hurt. He expects to be back at work in a few days.

This was one of a spate of accidents that have been occurring in the office in the last few months and I feel that it is time for some well-meant reminders.

(i)   Do not dawdle as you go about your work but there is no need to run, particularly when going up or down stairs, when passing dooorways, or turning blind corners.

(ii)   Electrical equipment in the office should be handled with care. Do not attempt to deal even with minor problems unless you have read the appropriate instruction manual; all faults should be reported immediately to Mr Tompkins, the office manager, who will willingly and promptly deal with them.

(iii)   All staff will be required to attend a brief lecture on health and safety in the office. These will be held each afternoon from next Monday and 30 staff may attend at any one time. I append a draft rota to cover all departments. Perhaps managers will let me know if they require any amendments.

(c)   The safety officer's entries in the accident book are shown in the right hand column of the book (on the previous pages).

Task 6

Peter and Mary Spratt
'Mari Celeste'
19 Duncan Drive
Epsom, Surrey

X E Dent Esq
Safety Officer
Duckley Ltd
Canardly Walk
London EC4A 9XJ

15th April 20X6

Dear Mr Dent,

Accident involving photocopier

I gather you spoke to my wife on the telephone earlier. As I believe she told you, not too much harm seems to have been caused by my accident yesterday although I still feel rather shaky and I am resting in bed at home.

For the record I should like to set down my understanding of what happened.

At about 10.30 am on 13 April I was walking down the third floor corridor in the direction of my office. I passed a young lady whom I believe is called Rachel. She appeared to be having difficulty with the photocopier. I am not sure what the model is but there was an identical one in my previous office and I frequently removed jammed paper from that one without coming to any harm.

I opened up the front of the photocopier and I could see the offending sheet inside. It was difficult to reach but not impossible and I started to tug at it.

I have no idea what happened after this. I woke up in hospital on Thursday afternoon. I was kept in 'for observation' and treated for shock, but was allowed to come home on Thursday evening.

So far as I am aware my actions were not dangerous in themselves. I am of the opinion that the photocopier is faulty. I trust that you will be having it inspected by a service engineer at the earliest opportunity.

Thank you again for your concern and please could you also thank anyone who gave assistance while I was unconscious. I hope I will be fit enough to return to work early next week.

Yours sincerely,

Peter Spratt

Peter Spratt

Task 7

Your answer will depend in part on your answers to previous tasks. Here is our suggestion. Yours should be consistent with any assumptions you made for tasks 5 and 6.

ACCIDENT INVESTIGATION QUESTIONNAIRE	
Name of injured person	MR PETER SPRATT
Date and time of accident	10 40 - 10 50 THURSDAY 13TH APRIL
Name of investigator	YOUR NAME
Date of investigation	14TH APRIL 19X6

Accident type

Exposure to explosion	**?**	Contact with electricity or electrical discharge	✓
Exposure to fire		Exposure to/contact with harmful substance	
Injured by animal		Contact with moving machinery	
Struck by vehicle		Injured while handling lifting or carrying	
Drowning or asphyxiation		Trapped by something collapsing or overturning	
Fall from height		Slip, trip or fall on same level	
Struck by moving object		Struck against something fixed or stationery	

Brief details of accident

MR SPRATT WAS ATTEMPTING TO REMOVE A PAPER JAM FROM THE PHOTOCOPIER AND APPEARS TO HAVE RECEIVED AN ELECTRIC SHOCK. HE WAS HOSPITALISED BRIEFLY AND IS NOW RECOVERING AT HOME.

Possible causes: please give, in order of importance, the code references of up to 5 possible causes (see the attached code sheet)

1 305	2 309	3 204	4 201	5 101

BPP PUBLISHING

DETAILED ENQUIRY			
	YES	NO	COMMENTS
Was the person injured carrying out a task that was part of their normal duties?		✓	MR TOMPKINS, THE OFFICE MANAGER, IS RESPONSIBLE FOR THE PHOTOCOPIER.
Was the person injured involved in an activity associated with work?	✓		APPEARS TO HAVE BEEN ASSISTING RACHEL PRESTON, WHO WAS PHOTOCOPYING PAPERS.
Was the person's immediate supervisor present in the area at the time of the accident?			NOT KNOWN.
If 'NO' state the location of the supervisor at the time and any specific instructions given by the supervisor prior to leaving the area.			-
Was the accident reported immediately?	✓		
If 'NO' state why there was a delay and how long the delay was.			-
To whom was the accident reported?	FIRST AID OFFICER, OFFICE MANAGER		
Has the task being performed been covered by a risk assessment?			NOT KNOWN. REFER TO SAFETY OFFICER.
Was the injured person specifically warned of the hazards of the task?			NOT KNOWN. UNLIKELY.
Was the person injured instructed to carry out the task?		✓	HE WAS VOLUNTARILY ASSISTING RACHEL PRESTON. NORMAL PROCEDURE IS TO CALL THE OFFICE MANAGER.
Was the task carried out in accordance with normal practice?		✓	SEE PREVIOUS ANSWER.
Was the task within the capability of the person injured?	✓		IN PRACTICE PAPER JAMS CAN NORMALLY BE REMOVED BY STAFF.
Was the person injured familiar with the type of plant/equipment/tools etc?	✓		IDENTICAL EQUIPMENT WAS USED IN HIS PREVIOUS JOB.
Had the person injured been trained to carry out the task safely?			NOT KNOWN IF TRAINED. HE CLAIMS TO HAVE REMOVED PAPER JAMS SAFELY IN THE PAST.

	YES	NO	COMMENTS
Was the task carried out by prescribed method?			*NOT KNOWN.*
Was protective clothing being worn?		✓	
Were any of the person's senses obscured/nullified which could have been a contributory factor?			*NOT KNOWN.*
Were plant/equipment/premises in normal condition?			*NOT KNOWN. HOWEVER MR TOMPKINS HAD TO CALL IN THE MAINTENANCE ENGINEER.*
Were guards/protective devices operating effectively?			*NOT KNOWN. SEE PREVIOUS ANSWER.*
Were warning notices displayed warning persons of hazards or to use protective clothing?			*THE PHOTOCOPIER HAS WARNING STICKERS DRAWING ATTENTION TO THE PRESENCE OF ELECTRICITY, BUT THESE ARE NOT PROMINENT.*
Was there a failure of service, component, plant or machinery?			*NOT KNOWN*
Is there a system for monitoring that procedures/instructions are followed?			*REFER TO SAFETY OFFICER, XAVIER DENT.*

Did any of the following environmental factors contribute to the accident?				
Rain	Snow	Ice	Fog	Cold
Humidity	Fumes	Gas	Vapour	Noise
Restricted space *POSSIBLY* ✓	Confined space *POSSIBLY* ✓	Uneven/unlevel surface	Condition of ground/floor	Radiation

Task 8

Hopefully this won't happen to you, but the scenario is drawn from genuine experiences.

It seems as if you are likely to strain a muscle if you attempt to do what is being asked of you. However, if you refuse to carry the bags you risk being labelled a 'wimp' and incurring the displeasure of your seniors. You are unlikely to win many friends if you complain to someone at a higher level that you are being picked on. If you simply give in and manage as best you can you will be seen as a soft touch.

This is a human relations problem really, but one that directly impinges on your health and safety. If you do yourself a serious injury you won't be able to travel to Bristol in any case.

Forget pride (male or female). Common sense is far rarer and far more admirable than physical strength. What you need to do in this situation is be assertive.

First reason with the person asking you to carry the bags. Explain as a simple fact that you are not physically able to do so. Do not accept arguments to the contrary, but suggest alternatives. ('I can't carry all of these, they're too heavy, so why don't we ...').

(a) You could ask to be allowed to claim taxi fares home this evening and to the station on Monday morning. This is probably more attractive than travelling by public transport, so you would be turning the situation to your advantage – brain over brawn!

(b) You could suggest that the load be spread amongst team members more evenly.

(c) You could suggest that some of the papers be left in the office: if they are not all needed on Day 1 they could be taken to Bristol later on, or perhaps sent by post.

(d) If you get nowhere with these suggestions you have little option but to speak to the team leader (who hopefully will have the maturity and authority to insist on option (b)).

Task 9

(a) Defence means things like locked doors and cabinets, security passes, indelible markings on assets, computer passwords, procedures for visitors, and the security conscious actions of staff.

(b) Detection is what happens if somebody manages to get through the defences (alarms ringing, security guards being called, searches being carried out of people leaving the building and so on).

(c) Deterrence is the combination of defences and detection systems: if people know that these exist they will not be tempted to try and break through the defences in the first place.

Task 10

(a) The main elements included in your diagram should be shown below. You have probably drawn something that looks similar to the place where you work, which is fine.

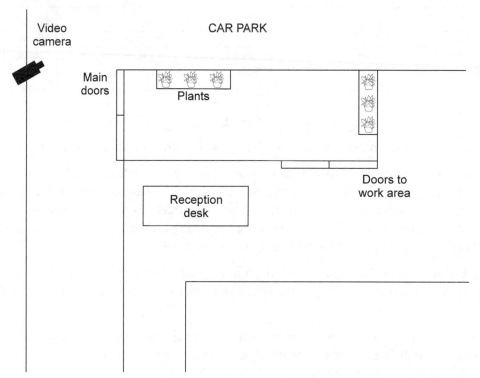

(b)

MEMO

To: Eleanor Martin
From: Carol Hunter
Subject: Security   Date: 2 June 20X6

As you are possibly aware, one of our courier's bikes was stolen from these premises yesterday evening. The courier admits that he did not lock his bike before leaving it unattended but the incident also shows up one or two problems in our own security procedures.

(i)   A person was loitering in our entrance lobby after office hours. It is not known who this person was, how he got on to the premises, or what he was doing or intending to do. The only thing that is reasonably certain is that he left on the courier's bike!

(ii)   It appears that there were no security guards on duty at all between 5.45pm and 6pm.

(iii)   The video camera overlooking our building is pointed at the car park. This is perhaps the most vulnerable area, but it means that security guards are totally unable to keep surveillance over the entrance to our building. Another camera, or a camera that sweeps from side to side is surely needed.

(iv)   The video was, in any case, switched off when the incident occurred 'to rewind the tape'. Would it not be preferable to have at least two tapes and keep the video running constantly? The current procedure leaves us in the position where we have no visual evidence of any incidents that occur between certain times.

(v)   Our security staff do not feel that they have any responsibility for the property of visitors to our premises. This may be the legal position but it is a highly anti-social attitude. I cannot see any reason for security staff to make a distinction and I am sure that all of our visitors, major customers and delivery people alike, would like to feel that they can visit us without placing themselves or their belongings at risk.

SOLUTION TO DEVOLVED ASSESSMENT 2: PORTFOLIO

Task 1

The answers will be specific to your own job and organisation so no solution is provided.

Task 2

(a)   and (b)

Obviously we do not know what your place of work looks like, but here is a diagram that shows what we had in mind. We suggest you keep a copy of your own version near at hand at work. Draw a fresh one if you change offices or if any of the information changes.

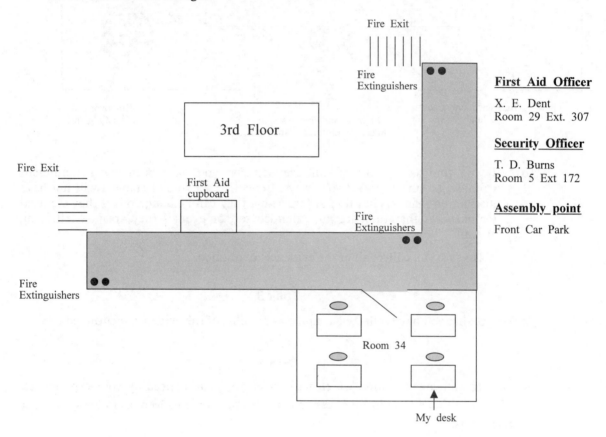

(c)   Again we cannot draw your work area, but the diagram on the next page is what we had in mind.

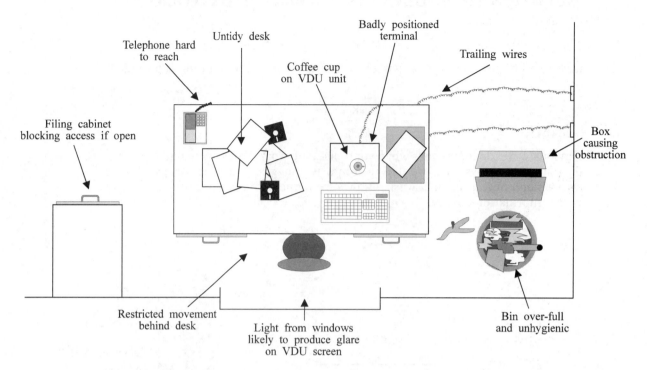

(d) If you find as a result of this exercise that you have been using equipment wrongly, be sure to mend your ways. Items like scissors or staplers will not have instruction manuals but do not forget that they can be dangerous if they are used for purposes that they are not intended for, or even if they are just left lying around.

(e) Make sure you collect all of the evidence mentioned.

Task 3

Make sure that you have collected as much as possible of the evidence mentioned.

Task 4

We ask for your own opinion which will of course be influenced by your experiences. During the author's time in practice the main *health* problems were as follows, in order of seriousness.

(a) Stress
(b) Tiredness
(c) Smoking and drinking (excess caffeine or alcohol or both)
(d) Lack of exercise
(e) Eye strain due to close figure work, VDU perils and so on (RSI, perhaps).
(f) Building-related problems such as poor ventilation, bad lighting, bad seating, etc.
(g) Minor office perils such as paper cuts
(h) Perils due to employee carelessness – bumping into others and the like

You might also have included travelling, harassment (sexual or otherwise) and a variety of other ailments related to sedentary work, such as weight problems or back pain.

Regarding security, accountants may be amongst the most at risk since they guard highly desirable assets such as cash and information.

Task 5

The HSE leaflet *Working with VDUs* has the following suggestions.

(a) Adjust your chair and VDU to find the most comfortable position for your work. As a broad guide, your arms should be approximately horizontal and your eyes at the same height as the top of the VDU casing.

(b) Make sure there is enough space underneath your desk to move your legs freely. Move any obstacles such as boxes or equipment.

(c) Avoid excess pressure on the backs of your legs and knees. A footrest, particularly for smaller users, may be helpful.

(d) Don't sit in the same position for long periods. Make sure you change your posture as often as practicable. Some movement is desirable, but avoid repeat stretching movements.

(e) Adjust your keyboard and screen to get a good keying and viewing position. A space in front of the keyboard is sometimes helpful for resting the hands and wrists while not keying.

(f) Don't bend your hands up at the wrist when keying. Try to keep a soft touch on the keys and don't overstretch your fingers. Good keyboard technique is important.

(g) Try different layouts of keyboard, screen and document holder to find the best arrangement for you.

(h) Make sure you have enough workspace to take whatever documents you need. A document holder may help you to avoid awkward neck movements.

(i) Arrange your desk and screen so that bright lights are not reflected in the screen. You shouldn't be directly facing windows or bright lights. Adjust curtains or blinds to prevent unwanted light.

(j) Make sure the characters on your screen are sharply focused and can be read easily. They shouldn't flicker or move.

(k) Make sure there are no layers of dirt, grime or finger marks on the screen.

(l) Use the brightness control on the screen to suit the lighting conditions in the room.

Task 6

Your answer will be specific to your own circumstances. Here is a fictional example of the sort of thing we had in mind.

(a) I experienced psychological problems at a time when there had been a number of changes in my personal circumstances.

    (i) My closest friend got married and left the area.

    (ii) A number of staff at work with whom I had had an extremely good relationship left to go to other jobs. I failed to make a serious effort to get to know their replacements.

    (iii) I was faced with the possibility of having to find £2,000 at short notice to pay off a debt.

    (iv) There was a temporary change in the management of the firm: my normal boss was sent on a secondment and I became directly responsible to my boss's boss.

(b) The uncertainty of my new social 'role' at work and the curtailment of social activities at home led to my becoming withdrawn and unsociable. I worked extremely long hours in the office and often took work home and continued in the evenings and at weekends.

The quality of my work did not suffer at all: in some ways I have never produced work of higher quality. However, I was working very inefficiently, often making false starts or following red herrings rather than concentrating on the matter in hand. This meant that work was often not finished by the deadline.

(c) My colleagues were undoubtedly affected by my problems. No action was taken to encourage me to meet deadlines, but a number of pieces of work were reallocated. At the time I felt no guilt about this, since in the past I had often helped out colleagues who were struggling to meet deadlines. In retrospect it is true to say that the work was not reallocated fairly by my temporary boss and, of course, it should not have had to be reallocated at all. My behaviour and its consequences was resented amongst my colleagues.

(d) The solution to the problem came about more by accident than design.

(i) I had a series of arguments with both colleagues and my temporary boss, during which the above came to light.

(ii) My social life at home improved as I moved into a new circle.

(iii) I took some time off work simply to relax. I came to terms with the fact that some of the criticisms that had been made of me were justified and that I was harming myself, my colleagues and my organisation by my attitude to work.

(e) Since the circumstances giving rise to the problems were largely personal, there is a limit to what could have been expected of the firm. The HSE leaflet advises that managers should be on the look out for indications of possible problems and includes the following general guidance.

> Intervention may simply consist of a timely, sympathetic enquiry regarding general health. When made by an acceptable person this may prevent distress from becoming a mental health problem. At this stage reassurance about job security and the confidentiality of discussion of personal problems is essential. It always helps to listen to what distressed people have to say.

In my situation the deadlines missed and the necessity to reallocate work were clear signs that all was not well. If this had been noticed by my employer action could have been a combination of sympathy and understanding together with closer than usual monitoring of my efficiency, and steps to ensure that I took account of the impact of my performance on others as well as myself.

(f) My responsibilities were to attempt not to allow personal difficulties to intrude upon my work (or at least to explain to my employer that all was not well) and in particular to work harder at relationships and consider the consequences of my actions for others.

Task 7

(a) Standard minimum contents are as follows. These will probably be listed on the lid of the box.

1	Guidance leaflet on first aid
20	Sterile adhesive dressings 'airstrip'
–	Sterile adhesive dressings 'elastoplast'
2	Sterile eye pad with bandage no. 16
6	Triangular bandage B.P. 90cm × 127cm
6	Safety pins
6	Sterile wound dressing medium no. 8
2	Sterile wound dressing large no. 9
3	Sterile wound dressing extra large no. 3
1	Person in charge notice, self-adhesive (this may be stuck up somewhere rather than in the box)

(b)   The box inspected at BPP Publishing was missing the plasters ('because people keep using them', according to the person in charge of the box!) and only had 4 safety pins and a paper clip. It had more than the minimum contents of some of the dressings. During the inspection the person in charge dropped the box on her foot!

(c)   The discrepancies should be reported to the person in charge of the box who should rectify them (for example replace the missing plasters and safety pins and remove the paper clip). There is, of course, no reason why a box should not contain more than the minimum number of standard items.

Task 8

To protect yourself you could take measures such as the following.

(a)   Follow organisational guidelines about personal safety and security to the letter.

(b)   Avoid doing things that might provoke people. These could include, for example, being insensitive (wearing a £500 Armani suit to work when you spend much of the day dealing with people living in poverty, say); descending to abusive language if people start swearing at you; allowing yourself to be distracted by telephone calls or other demands on your attention that make the person you are dealing with feel that he or she is not being taken seriously; being inconsistent or showing favouritism (bending the rules for one customer but not for the next).

If you can think of more specific things that would upset the people you deal with in your job, be sure to note them down.

(c)   Don't take unnecessary risks. If a customer asks you out for a drink, say, refuse if you are at all unsure of them. If you are tempted to agree, meet in a public place, make sure someone knows you are going, don't give them personal information like your address and phone number until you are sure of them.

(d)   Seek assistance from colleagues or security staff if an interviewee starts to become threatening.

(e)   Don't be violent or aggressive in manner towards your customer: an obvious point, but worth making.

Your employer could take the following measures.

(a)   Provide you with training in dealing with difficult situations.

(b)   Provide you with protection by arranging the working environment in such a way that it would be physically difficult to assault you. The obvious example is the counters and screens in banks and post offices. Modern systems have armour plated screens that are not normally on view but which can rise up and seal off staff from the public area in less than a second.

(c)   Not place you in situations that are likely to lead to aggression. One example would be abandoning petty bureaucratic rules that just annoy people. Another would be providing whatever it is that people are paying for to the required standard (assaults on public transport staff, for example, may ultimately be due to the failure of the public transport managers to provide a good service).

Neither of these answers is exhaustive. You may well have thought of other examples form personal experience.

If you really are in this situation you may be interested to know that the Suzy Lamplugh Trust has produced a *Guide to Personal Safety at Work* which gives advice on developing confidence, assessing and reducing risks, dealing with aggression and physical attack, and travelling safely outside the workplace.

Task 9

The contract of employment contains a confidentiality clause. If you do not keep the affairs of the company secret you are in breach of contract.

In practice this is unlikely to mean that you have to clam up even if your partner asks what sort of a day you have had at work. However the clause would certainly operate if it were discovered that you had leaked internal information to somebody that could misuse it for their own advantage and/or to the detriment of the company.

This contract also requires that if you leave the company you must surrender any of the company's records that are in your possession and anybody else's records that you have on behalf of your company, for example the cash book of a client that you were working on. This is quite a common position for an accountant working for a firm of accountants to be in, so you may well have a clause like this in your own contract.

The second clause in the contract entitles the company to search you, your bag and your locker and so on. The company has no general right to do this unless there is such a clause in your contract.

As for the notice, if it is displayed prominently, so that people entering the building can see it, it entitles the company to search anyone entering or leaving the premises. The notice alone would not give the employer the right to search an employee's locker.

Task 10

(a)   You may have seen an article in the newspaper a while ago that showed the effects on spiders' web-spinning abilities of various drugs. Caffeine came off worse than marijuana and speed, leaving spiders incapable of spinning anything better than a few threads strung together at random. Only sleeping pills did worse than caffeine, because the spiders dropped off before they got started.

Here is a possible notice based on the article reproduced in the question.

DO YOU NEED THAT CUP OF COFFEE?

Medical research shows that the effects of caffeine are ....

an inability to concentrate

poor decision making

irritability

nervousness

forgetfulness

fatigue

insomnia

In some people caffeine causes an accentuation of pre-menstrual syndrome and diarrhoea.

Fancy a cup of ...... water?

Parts (b), (c), and (d) will have answers specific to you.

If it is of any interest, the author of this task, a confirmed caffeine addict, tried this experiment, noticed only withdrawal symptoms and gave up. However, in many ways this merely confirms the findings of the research: poor decision making, inability to concentrate (on giving up coffee) etc!

Task 11

An example of a real scheme will allow you to judge how good your answer was. This is taken from a work environment far more likely to encounter safety problems than the average accounts office, but it illustrates the principles.

On the construction site of its new research centre Glaxo, the pharmaceuticals company, had a scheme whereby prizes such as a car were raffled as rewards for safe working. The safety record of the site was ten times better than the national average.

(a) The target was a million man-hours without losing time through serious injury: this took about three months. (Time without injury targets are sensible: the time will depend on the number of workers.) There were also monthly league tables measuring things such as safe working systems, and attitudes amongst different parts of the workforce.

(b) Once this was achieved a prize draw was held at a feast to which the whole workforce was invited, underlining the importance attached to safety by management and allaying suspicions that the draw might be a fix.

(c) Everyone currently on the workforce had an equal chance of winning, even if they had only been employed for a few weeks. This meant that short-term workers had the same incentive to work safely as others. Other companies with more stable workforces have schemes allowing individuals to build up safety merit points that can be exchanged for gifts of varying value like holidays and store vouchers.

(d) The main prize was a car and there were six runners up prizes of £4,000 each. Obviously the size of the prize would depend on the size of the organisation. There were also daily spot prizes of £10: these were awarded by safety personnel to any worker who was observed carrying out their duties with a high regard to safety or taking steps to remove some potential hazard (eg reporting a hazard). There was also a monthly quiz with prizes worth up to £100.

(e) The rules were strictly applied. Even a relatively trivial accident could result in the clock being set back to zero. This happened for example when a worker had to take more than three days off work after tripping on some steps on his way to the toilet. Some distinction clearly has to be made between absences due to things that happen at work and those due to things that happen outside work.

Task 12

The first document is a fire extinguisher inspection report. The extinguisher on the fifth floor rear stairs needs to be replaced (in fact it should have been replaced following the previous visit). The document is dated 19X2. A further inspection is long overdue. It would probably be worth looking at the extinguishers in your own area for any obvious signs of faults and reporting them if you find any. This may not be particularly easy to do, since you are unlikely to be trained to do so, but if you see something leaking or obviously damaged, or if you pick up an extinguisher and it feels empty this should certainly be mentioned.

The second two documents are a fire alarm and emergency lighting test reports. The first (13.4.X6) suggests that two emergency lights need to be repaired: presumably this is why the 'further visit required' box is ticked, since nothing seems to have been done on this visit. The main supply cupboard also seems to need repairs.

The final document suggests that the 7th floor emergency lighting needs repairs and perhaps calls into further question the safety of the mains supply.

Task 13

You should not under any circumstances operate the paper shredding machine, even if instructed to do so.

There is not a great deal that you as an employee can do about this - in practice you are not likely to have access to such documents and we are not suggesting that you should spy on your employer. It is your duty to report any possible hazards though, so if it is ages since the last fire drill and the alarms are never tested, it is worth pointing this out to whoever is responsible. If you use a PC or some other electrical equipment, has it ever been tested for electrical safety?

You should draw the notice to the attention of anyone you see operating the machine and any other colleagues *likely* to try to use the machine.

Index

BPP PUBLISHING

Index

ORDER FORM

Any books from our AAT range can be ordered by telephoning 020-8740-2211. Alternatively, send this page to our address below, fax it to us on 020-8740-1184, or email us at **publishing@bpp.com.** Or look us up on our website: www.bpp.com

We aim to deliver to all UK addresses inside 5 working days; a signature will be required. Order to all EU addresses should be delivered within 6 working days. All other orders to overseas addresses should be delivered within 8 working days.

To: BPP Publishing Ltd, Aldine House, Aldine Place, London W12 8AW

Tel: 020-8740 2211   **Fax: 020-8740 1184**   **Email: publishing@bpp.com**

Mr / Ms (full name): _____

Daytime delivery address: _____

_____

Postcode: _____   Daytime Tel: _____

Please send me the following quantities of books.

	5/00 Interactive Text	8/00 DA Kit	8/00 CA Kit
FOUNDATION			
Unit 1 Recording Income and Receipts	☐	☐	
Unit 2 Making and Recording Payments	☐	☐	
Unit 3 Ledger Balances and Initial Trial Balance	☐	☐	
Unit 4 Supplying information for Management Control	☐	☐	
Unit 20 Working with Information Technology (8/00 Text)	☐		
Unit 22/23 Achieving Personal Effectiveness	☐		
INTERMEDIATE			
Unit 5 Financial Records and Accounts	☐	☐	
Unit 6 Cost Information	☐	☐	
Unit 7 Reports and Returns	☐	☐	
Unit 21 Using Information Technology	☐		
Unit 22: see below			
TECHNICIAN			
Unit 8/9 Core Managing Costs and Allocating Resources	☐		☐
Unit 10 Core Managing Accounting Systems	☐	☐	
Unit 11 Option Financial Statements (Accounting Practice)	☐		☐
Unit 12 Option Financial Statements (Central Government)	☐		☐
Unit 15 Option Cash Management and Credit Control	☐	☐	
Unit 16 Option Evaluating Activities	☐	☐	
Unit 17 Option Implementing Auditing Procedures	☐	☐	
Unit 18 Option Business Tax FA00(8/00 Text)	☐	☐	
Unit 19 Option Personal Tax FA00(8/00 Text)	☐	☐	
TECHNICIAN 1999			
Unit 17 Option Business Tax Computations FA99 (8/99 Text & Kit)	☐	☐	
Unit 18 Option Personal Tax Computations FA99 (8/99 Text & Kit)	☐	☐	
TOTAL BOOKS	☐	+ ☐	+ ☐ = ☐

Postage and packaging:

UK: £2.00 for each book to maximum of £10

                                                                    └ @ £9.95 each = £ ☐

Europe (inc ROI and Channel Islands): £4.00 for first book, £2.00 for each extra   P & P   £ ☐

Rest of the World: £20.00 for first book, £10 for each extra

Unit 22 Maintaining a Healthy Workplace Interactive Text (postage free)   ☐ @ £3.95   £ ☐

                                                            GRAND TOTAL £ ☐

I enclose a cheque for £ _____ (cheques to BPP Publishing Ltd) or charge to Mastercard/Visa/Switch

Card number ☐☐☐☐ ☐☐☐☐ ☐☐☐☐ ☐☐☐☐ ☐☐☐☐

Start date _____   **Expiry date** _____   **Issue no. (Switch only)**___

Signature _____

REVIEW FORM & FREE PRIZE DRAW

All original review forms from the entire BPP range, completed with genuine comments, will be entered into one of two draws on 31 January 2001 and 31 July 2001. The names on the first four forms picked out on each occasion will be sent a cheque for £50.

Name: _____   Address: _____

_____

_____

How have you used this Interactive Text?
(Tick one box only)

☐ Home study (book only)

☐ On a course: college _____

☐ With 'correspondence' package

☐ Other _____

Why did you decide to purchase this Interactive Text? *(Tick one box only)*

☐ Have used BPP Texts in the past

☐ Recommendation by friend/colleague

☐ Recommendation by a lecturer at college

☐ Saw advertising

☐ Other _____

During the past six months do you recall seeing/receiving any of the following?
(Tick as many boxes as are relevant)

☐ Our advertisement in *Accounting Technician* magazine

☐ Our advertisement in *Pass*

☐ Our brochure with a letter through the post

Which (if any) aspects of our advertising do you find useful?
(Tick as many boxes as are relevant)

☐ Prices and publication dates of new editions

☐ Information on Interactive Text content

☐ Facility to order books off-the-page

☐ None of the above

Have you used the companion Assessment Kit for this subject?   ☐ Yes   ☐ No

Your ratings, comments and suggestions would be appreciated on the following areas

	Very useful	Useful	Not useful
Introductory section (How to use this Interactive Text etc)	☐	☐	☐
Chapter topic lists	☐	☐	☐
Chapter learning objectives	☐	☐	☐
Key terms	☐	☐	☐
Assessment alerts	☐	☐	☐
Examples	☐	☐	☐
Activities and answers	☐	☐	☐
Key learning points	☐	☐	☐
Quick quizzes and answers	☐	☐	☐
List of key terms and index	☐	☐	☐
Icons	☐	☐	☐

	Excellent	Good	Adequate	Poor
Overall opinion of this Text	☐	☐	☐	☐

Do you intend to continue using BPP Interactive Texts/Assessment Kits? ☐ Yes ☐ No

Please note any further comments and suggestions/errors on the reverse of this page.

Please return to: Nick Weller, BPP Publishing Ltd, FREEPOST, London, W12 8BR

REVIEW FORM & FREE PRIZE DRAW (continued)

Please note any further comments and suggestions/errors below

FREE PRIZE DRAW RULES

1   Closing date for 31 January 2001 draw is 31 December 2000. Closing date for 31 July 2001 draw is 30 June 2001.

2   Restricted to entries with UK and Eire addresses only. BPP employees, their families and business associates are excluded.

3   No purchase necessary. Entry forms are available upon request from BPP Publishing. No more than one entry per title, per person. Draw restricted to persons aged 16 and over.

4   Winners will be notified by post and receive their cheques not later than 6 weeks after the relevant draw date.

5   The decision of the promoter in all matters is final and binding. No correspondence will be entered into.